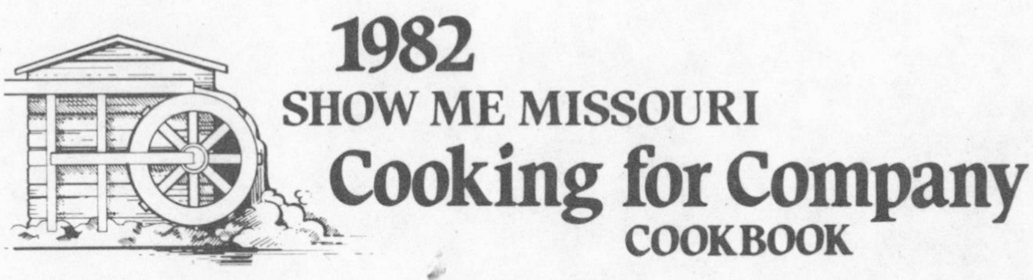

The American Cancer Society
Missouri Division, Inc.

The American Cancer Society, Missouri Division, Inc. has no reason to doubt that recipe ingredients, instructions, and directions will work successfully. However, the ingredients, instructions and directions have not necessarily been thoroughly or systematically tested, and the cook should not hesitate to test and question procedures and directions before preparation. The recipes in this book have been collected from various sources, and neither The American Cancer Society, Missouri Division, Inc., nor any contributor, publisher, printer, distributor or seller of this book is responsible for errors or omissions.

First Printing, 35,000, 1981

International Standard Book Number 0-939114-23-2

Printed in the United States of America
Wimmer Brothers Fine Printing & Lithography
Memphis, Tennessee 38118

"Cookbooks of Distinction"™

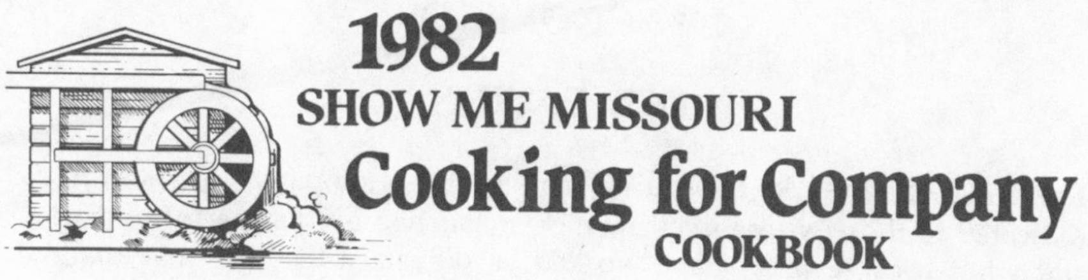

The 1982 "Cooking for Company" Cookbook, the third in the series of Show Me Missouri cookbooks, has been published as a fund-raising project of the Missouri Division of the American Cancer Society.

We wish to thank all who participated in the preparation of this book, and those who shared their special recipes with us. Only through the dedicated efforts of the multitude of volunteers with the battle against cancer by won, and the dream of a cancer-free world become a reality.

Our deepest gratitude to you who have made a contribution to the American Cancer Society through the purchase of this book.

Mrs. Margaret Lawlor
Chairman

1982 COOKBOOK

DEDICATION

The 1982 "Show Me Missouri Cooking for Company" Cookbook is dedicated to those whose lives have been touched by the specter of cancer and who, because of it, have worked so diligently to erase that shadow from the lives of others.

TABLE OF CONTENTS

BATTLE OF ATHENS

On August 5, 1861, Athens, Missouri, suffered a 2-hour battle, known as the Battle of Athens, the northernmost such battle of the Civil War west of the Mississippi.

Early on the morning of the 5th, Union Colonel David Moore, with only 400 men and two Home Guard units from Keokuk, Iowa, met Colonel Martin Green of Lewis County, Missouri, backed by a 1500-man regiment and a Confederate Home Guard. Green committed some tactical errors at the onset of the conflict, attacking with his men spread over several miles and then opening fire with cannons. One of these struck the door frame of the Joseph Benning home (pictured to the left), narrowly missing the family eating breakfast at the dining room table.

With the aid of the calvary from Alexandria, Missouri, led by Major Callahan, Moore's broken regiment led a successful bayonet assault against Green. It ended in a full Confederate retreat, with Moore's men capturing supplies, horses and several guns. Fourteen Confederates and three Union soldiers died during this battle, which also left 43 injured.

At that time, Athens was a thriving river town with a population of 400; today there are less than eight families in this Civil War ghost town. In 1975 Athens was made a state park, and the Joseph Benning home, the John Smith house, and Moore's headquarters during the attack have been preserved for the public.

Appetizers

POINTE COUPEE PARISH SHRIMP DIP

½ cup butter
2 bunches shallots, chopped fine
6 ripe tomatoes, dipped in boiling water and skinned
1 bunch parsley, chopped fine
2 large cans mushroom stems and pieces
Dry sherry as desired
Small amount of flour
5 pounds shrimp
Salt and pepper to taste
Whipping cream as desired

Melt butter; wilt shallots in the butter. Add tomatoes and cook until blended into a paste. Add parsley and mushrooms; cook. Add dry sherry to taste. Thicken with flour by making a paste of flour and mushroom liquid. Add shrimp. Add seasoning. When ready to serve, add whipping cream. Keep warm and serve.

Mrs. Howard Hill
Ray County (Richmond)

SALLY'S RAW VEGETABLE DIP

1 cup mayonnaise
½ teaspoon lemon juice
¼ teaspoon salt
½ cup sour cream
¼ teaspoon paprika
⅛ teaspoon curry powder
½ teaspoon Worcestershire sauce
1 minced clove garlic
1 teaspoon Spice Island "Fine Herbes"

Add all ingredients in mixing bowl. Stir well with spoon or wire whisk. Do not use electric mixer. Refrigerate until ready to serve. *Makes 1½ cups. An excellent dip for any raw vegetable.*

Sally Wasserman
Warren County (Warrenton)

RAW VEGETABLE DIP

1 (8-ounce) carton sour cream
1 cup Miracle Whip
1 teaspoon dill weed
1 teaspoon onion, finely chopped
1 teaspoon dried parsley flakes
1 teaspoon Beau Monde seasoning
Dash of onion salt

Combine ingredients. Mix thoroughly. Refrigerate for 24 hours before serving. *Serve with raw vegetables.*

Mrs. Milford Ritterbusch (Elma)
Gasconade County — Gasconade South Unit (Owensville)

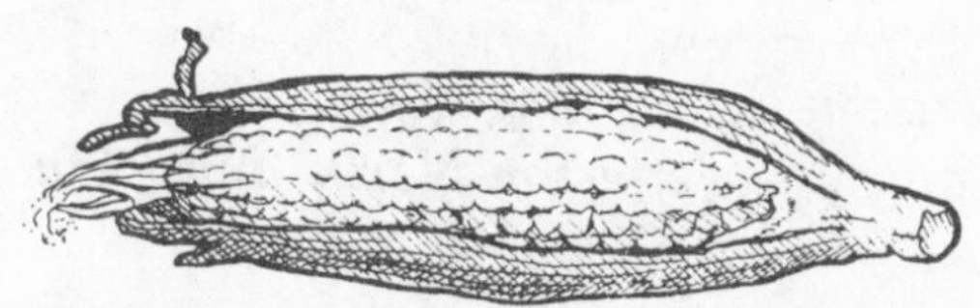

CHILI CHEESE DIP

1 pound lean ground beef
1 pound processed American cheese, cut into small pieces
1 (8 to 10 ounce) can green chilies and tomatoes
2 teaspoons Worcestershire sauce
½ teaspoon chili powder

Brown ground beef well and drain off excess fat. Put ground beef and all remaining ingredients in a slow cooker; stir well. Cover and cook on high for 1 hour, stirring until cheese is fully melted. Serve immediately or turn to low for serving up to 6 hours later. Serve with tortilla or corn chips. *This recipe may be doubled for larger slow cookers. For thicker dip: stir in a paste of 2 tablespoons flour and 3 tablespoons water. This is an excellent dip for parties.*

Mrs. David DeFrain (Donna)
Johnson County (Warrensburg)

PRETTY OLIVE DIP

2 (8-ounce) packages cream cheese
2 (3½-ounce) packages dried smoked beef
½ cup chopped green stuffed olives
¼ cup mayonnaise
2 tablespoons dry vermouth or sherry (optional)
½ teaspoon chopped onion

In a large bowl, combine ingredients. Mix until well blended. Mixture will be thick and sticky. Refrigerate until ready to serve. Serve with crackers. *This recipe lends itself to seasonal activities. It can easily be molded into Christmas tree with olive slices as ornaments, for example.*

Laura Robertson
Jefferson County — Jefferson North Unit (Arnold)

RYE BREAD DIP

1 (8-ounce) package cream cheese
1 (12-ounce) carton sour cream
¾ cup mayonnaise
¼ cup chopped green onion tops
¼ cup parsley, chopped
2 teaspoons dill weed
4 teaspoons Beau Monde
2 teaspoons garlic salt

Combine ingredients into creamy consistency. Have 2 unsliced round rye breads set aside. Cut center out of 1 and fill cavity with dip. Break second loaf and removed center from first loaf into dipping-sized pieces. Arrange pieces around dip-filled bread on platter. Sprinkle with parsley. *Yield: 17 to 20 servings.*

Debbie Baker
Jefferson County — Jefferson North Unit (Barnhardt)

CUCUMBER DIP

Juice of ½ lemon
1 (12-ounce) package cream cheese, softened
2 green onions, with tops
¾ teaspoon salt
Dash of cayenne
1 large cucumber, peeled

Place ingredients in blender. Process until thoroughly blended. Strain pulp afterwards for seeds. Chill. *Serve as dip with raw vegetables.*

Susan Mangrum
Boone Unit (Columbia)

When making ice cubes for a party, place twists of lemon or lime in tray sections for decorative ice cubes.

CHILI DIP

1 pound ground beef, cooked and drained
½ cup chopped onion
⅔ cup hot catsup
1 tablespoon chili powder
1 teaspoon cumin
1 teaspoon salt
1 can red beans, mashed in liquid

Combine all ingredients. Simmer for 20 minutes, let set for 2½ hours. *Warm to serve with corn chips to dip. This may be also used for sloppy joes or coney dogs.*

Donna Clark
Hickory County (Wheatland)

CORNED BEEF CHEESE BALL

3 (8-ounce) packages cream cheese
1 bunch green onions, chopped (including tops)
1 tablespoon MSG
1 tablespoon Worcestershire sauce
½ teaspoon salt
2 packages corned beef, chopped

Combine all ingredients, except ⅓ cup corned beef. Shape into a ball. Cover with remaining corned beef. *This is very good with party crackers.*

June Fricke
Gasconade County — Gasconade South Unit (Hermann)

CHICKEN LIVER PATE

1 pound fresh or frozen chicken livers, thawed
Butter or margarine
3 tablespoons mayonnaise
2 teaspoons lemon juice
2 tablespoons butter, softened
1 tablespoon finely chopped onion
8 to 10 drops bottled hot pepper sauce
½ teaspoon salt
½ teaspoon dry mustard
Dash pepper

Cook livers, covered in small amount of butter or margarine, stirring occasionally until no longer pink. Put meat in meat grinder; blend with remaining ingredients. Place mixture in a mold. Chill several hours; carefully remove mold. *Garnish with chopped, hard-cooked egg or snipped chives or parsley. Serve with crackers.*

Delores Grannemann
Gasconade County — Gasconade South Unit (Hermann)

CHEESE BALL

2 (8-ounce) packages cream cheese, softened
2 packages pressed chipped beef
1 bunch chopped green onions with tops
1 tablespoon MSG
1 tablespoon Worcestershire sauce
1 small jar pimientos

While cheese is softening, reserve 4 slices chipped beef for top; finely chop the remainder. Combine cream cheese, chopped chipped beef, green onions, MSG, Worcestershire and pimientos. Mix well. Form into a ball. Chill 2 hours. *Serve with snack crackers.*

Nancy Stuart
Audrain County (Mexico)

MOULES MARINIERE

5 pounds mussels, cleaned
1 cup chopped parsley
1 cup dry white wine
½ cup unsalted butter
3 tablespoons chopped shallots
1 teaspoon salt
1 teaspoon freshly ground pepper
6 tablespoons heavy cream

Combine all ingredients except cream and simmer for 5 minutes. Remove mussels; add cream and heat about 5 minutes; return mussels to pot and heat. Remove and serve at once. *Garnish with chopped parsley.*

Anthony's Restaurant (Anthony M. Bennito)
St. Louis County — Central County Unit (St. Louis)

SUMMER SAUSAGE

5 pounds ground beef
2½ teaspoons coarse ground pepper
2½ teaspoons garlic powder
3 whole peppercorns
2 teaspoons liquid smoke
5 rounded teaspoons curing salt
2½ teaspoons mustard seed

Combine all ingredients, cover and place in refrigerator. Take out and mix for several minutes on the second, third and fourth days. Fifth day, take out and place on a board, divide into 4 or 5 rolls. Pat down to remove all air bubbles. Form into logs and place on broiler rack or any rack in shallow pan. Bake as follows: 1 hour at 140 degrees, 45 minutes at 200 degrees, 1 hour at 140 degrees, 45 minutes at 200 degrees, 1 hour at 140 degrees, 45 minutes at 200 degrees. Turn oven off. Leave in oven 1 hour. Turn every 15 minutes while baking, blotting with paper towels. Wrap and refrigerate or freeze until needed.

Mrs. Conrad Van Camp (Geneva)
Dallas County (Louisburg)

Similar recipe submitted by:
Terry Sites
Daviess County (Gallatin)

Clean plastic egg cartons can serve as extra ice makers for parties.

WATER CHESTNUT WRAPS

Whole, canned water chestnuts
Bacon

Wrap each water chestnut with half slice of bacon and stick a toothpick through center. Bake on cookie sheet at 350 degrees for 15 to 20 minutes until bacon is brown.

Sweet and sour sauce:

⅔ cup brown sugar
2 tablespoons catsup
1 teaspoon prepared mustard
1 teaspoon soy sauce
1 teaspoon Worcestershire sauce
1 teaspoon butter

Put all ingredients in saucepan and stir well. Warm over low to medium heat and then move to serving dish or fondue pot, with bacon-wrapped water chestnuts surrounding sauce on platter. *Add a little water to sauce, if needed, to thin. If you haven't tried these yet, you'll love 'em.*

Debbie Petersimes
St. Louis County — West County Unit (St. Louis)

SAUSAGE BALLS

2 pounds hot sausage
6 cups biscuit mix
2 packages soft Cheddar cheese

Work the 3 ingredients together. Shape into 1-inch balls. Bake at 325 degrees for 8 to 10 minutes. *Best when served warm. Will make approximately 8 dozen sausage balls. Delicious and tasty, and quick and easy to prepare.*

Marilyn Brodmerkle
Livingston County (Chillicothe)

OREGON COUNTY — GREER SPRINGS

Early settlers in Oregon County often built their homesites near springs, usually their only source of water. Many of these served several neighboring settlers and the larger ones usually boasted mills that ground wheat and corn to aid the pioneers' struggle for survival. Some have become landmarks and still retain part of the mill equipment, although none is currently operable. One of the best known of these springs was Greer, the second largest spring in Missouri, with an average daily flow of 187,000,000 gallons. The first mill was located at the bottom of the steep valley where the spring issues. A second was built half a mile above the spring and was operated by using a complicated system of cables and wheels to transfer the motion of the large waterwheel to the new mill on top of the ridge.

With the decline of farming and the shift of population, the mill closed about 1920 and the system was demolished, but the old mill building still stands and Greer Spring is still as wild and beautiful as it was in the 1800s.

Breakfast/Brunch

IMPOSSIBLE QUICHE

12 slices bacon, cooked and crumbled
1 cup shredded Swiss cheese
½ cup chopped onion
2 cups milk
½ cup biscuit mix
4 eggs
¼ teaspoon salt
¼ teaspoon pepper

Sprinkle crumbled bacon, cheese and onion in greased 9-inch pie pan. Combine milk, biscuit mix, eggs, salt and pepper and blend at high speed for 1 minute. Pour this over other ingredients in pan. Bake at 350 degrees for 50 to 55 minutes. Let stand 5 minutes before serving. *Serves 5.*

Mrs. Robert Carney (LaBurns)
Phelps County (Rolla)

Similar recipe submitted by:
Mary Louise Ahmann
St. Charles County (St. Charles)
Variation: Instead of biscuit mix, use a frozen deep dish pastry shell.

Nicolette Papanek
Miller County (Eldon)

Allow egg whites to come to room temperature before whipping for greater volume.

AMAZING QUICHE

12 slices bacon
1 cup Cheddar cheese, shredded
½ cup onion, finely chopped
2 cups milk
½ cup buttermilk baking mix
4 eggs
¼ teaspoon salt
⅛ teaspoon pepper

Fry bacon until crisp. Drain and crumble. Lightly grease 9 inch to 10 inch pie plate. Combine bacon, cheese and onion. Spread in pie plate. Combine remaining ingredients in blender and process for 1 minute. Pour over pie plate. Bake at 350 degrees for 50 to 55 minutes, or until knife inserted in center comes out clean. Cool 5 minutes before slicing and serving.

JoAnn Kinder
St. Louis County — North Central Unit (Florissant)

CHEESE STRATA

8 slices bread
¼ cup butter or margarine, softened
2½ cups American cheese, diced
4 eggs, lightly beaten
2½ cups milk
1 teaspoon salt
¼ teaspoon dry mustard

Trim crusts from bread. Butter bread and cut each slice into quarters. Alternate layers of bread and cheese in 12-x-8-inch baking dish with cheese on top. Combine remaining ingredients. Mix well and pour over cheese and bread. Cover and chill overnight or at least 6 hours. Bake at 325 for 45 minutes or until firm. Let stand 5 minutes before serving. *Cut into squares to serve.*

Dorothy C. Long
Pemiscot County (Braggadocio)

CHICKEN AMANDINE QUICHE

1 unbaked deep dish pastry shell, or 2 regular 9-inch shells
2 tablespoons reconstituted minced dried onion or ¼ cup fresh onion
1 (5-ounce) can chicken, diced or ½ to ⅔ cup cooked chicken
¼ cup sliced almonds
6 ounces shredded Swiss cheese, about 1½ cups
3 eggs, slightly beaten
1½ cups milk
½ teaspoon salt
½ teaspoon mace, basil or thyme
⅛ teaspoon pepper
About 2 tablespoons grated Parmesan cheese

Spread onion on bottom of pastry shell. (To reconstitute dried onion, add water to cover onion until pieces are plumped up, about 10 minutes.) If not using deep dish pastry, divide onion evenly between 2 shells. Top with layers of chicken, almonds and cheese, in that order. Combine eggs, milk, salt, herbs and pepper. Pour liquid mixture over layered ingredients in shell. Sprinkle Parmesan cheese over top. Bake at 375 degrees for 30 to 40 minutes or until knife inserted near center comes out clean. Allow to stand 10 minutes before cutting and serving 6 to 8. *Note: Place pastry shells on cookie sheet placed on oven shelf before pouring liquid mixture over layered ingredients. This avoids spills. Amounts given are generous for deep dish shell and should be divided between 2 shallow shells. Allow 5 to 10 minutes additional baking time for deep dish pastry shell. This is an elegant, filling brunch, lunch or (with a crisp green salad) supper dish and easy to do with pantry shelf ingredients.*

Polly Paulus
St. Louis County — Central County Unit (Clayton)

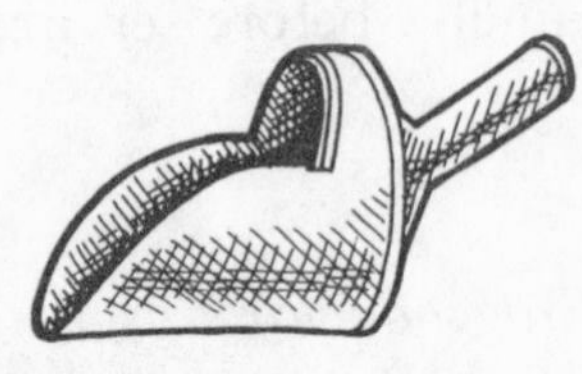

HAM AND MUSHROOM QUICHE

3 eggs
1 cup Swiss cheese, shredded
1½ cups milk
¼ teaspoon salt
⅛ teaspoon pepper
½ cup Bisquick
½ cup ham, cut into ½-inch cubes
1 (4-ounce) can mushroom pieces, drained
¼ cup margarine, melted

Beat eggs until light. Combine with remaining ingredients. Pour into greased 9-inch pie plate. Bake at 350 for 45 minutes to 1 hour.

Elaine Deppermann
Gasconade County - Gasconade South Unit (Owensville)

CHEESE PUFFS

White sandwich bread
Grated Parmesan cheese
Grated or minced onion, just enough to flavor well
Salad dressing or mayonnaise
Additional parmesan cheese

Cut small rounds from sandwich bread, taking care to leave no crust. Mix cheese and onion; add salad dressing or mayonnaise to moisten. Spread on bread rounds. Use enough to make a slightly mounded puff. Sprinkle with Parmesan cheese lightly over top. Place under broiler and brown lightly. *This recipe came from a dear friend and to paraphrase Will Rogers, "I never saw a man (or woman) who didn't like them."*

Ramona Kitchen
Oregon County (Alton)

SOUTHERN HOT FRUIT

1 (20-ounce) can pineapple rings
1 (29-ounce) can peach slices or halves
1 (29-ounce) can pears
1 (17-ounce) can apricots
1 (10 or 14-ounce) jar Musselman's red spiced apple rings
1 cup combined fruit juice
½ cup sugar
2 tablespoons flour
½ cup butter or margarine

Drain the 5 fruits well and arrange in a large casserole dish, at least 12-x-12-x-3-inch. Combine fruit juice, sugar, flour and margarine in a saucepan. Cook over medium heat until thick. Pour over the drained fruit. Cover casserole and let set overnight in the refrigerator. Just before serving, heat at 350 degrees for 30 minutes. *Serves 16. This recipe is especially good served with ham or turkey. It can be served with coffee cake or rolls for Christmas or Easter breakfast.*

Mrs. Ben L. Barton (Pauline)
Taney County (Branson)

Use an egg slicer for uniform slices of mushrooms.

WAFFLES

2 cups flour
1 tablespoon baking powder
1 teaspoon salt
2 tablespoon sugar
2 eggs, beaten
1¾ cups milk
5 tablespoons melted shortening

Sift dry ingredients. Mix eggs and milk together, then add to dry ingredients. Add melted shortening. Bake in waffle iron according to directions. Top with butter and syrup. *Note: For a more festive meal, top waffles with warm blueberry (or other fruit) pie filling. Garnish with whipped cream and a couple of blueberries. For a lighter waffle, separate eggs. Mix egg yolks with milk; beat whites until soft peaks form. Fold into batter. Remaining batter can be baked, frozen, and reheated in microwave or toaster as needed.*

Nancy Summers
Holt County (Maitland)

GINNA'S GARLIC CHEESE GRITS

1 cup grits
4 cups water
2 rolls Kraft garlic cheese
½ cup margarine
1 teaspoon garlic powder
2 eggs
Milk

Cook grits in water as directed on package. To cooked grits add garlic cheese, margarine and garlic powder. Put eggs in a measuring cup and beat. Add milk to make 1 cup. Mix all together; bake in a 9-inch square pan at 300 degrees for 45 minutes. May be topped with shredded cheese in final minutes of cooking, if desired.

Mrs. Gene Copeland
New Madrid County (New Madrid)

EGG BRUNCH

12 eggs
¾ cup milk
1 teaspoon salt
7 tablespoons butter, divided
½ cup flour
1 quart milk
Pepper to taste
4 slices bacon, quartered
3 small jars dried beef, cut into bite-size pieces
1 or 2 small cans mushrooms, drained

In skillet, scramble eggs, milk and salt in 3 tablespoons butter. Set aside. Melt remaining butter in saucepan, add flour and slowly add milk to make sauce. Cook over medium heat until thick. Stir frequently. Add bacon, pepper, beef and mushrooms, reserving a few mushrooms for top. Put ½ the sauce in a buttered 9-x-12-inch baking pan. Add eggs and then remaining sauce. Top with reserved mushrooms. Bake 1 hour at 275 degrees. *This can be made ahead and refrigerated before baking. Excellent for company breakfast because everything is ready all at once and clean up is easy.*

Sharon Peacock
Dade County (Lockwood)

OATMEAL PANCAKES

1½ cups quick cooking oatmeal
½ cup flour, unsifted
1 teaspoon salt
1 teaspoon baking soda
1 tablespoon sugar
3 tablespoons vegetable oil
2 cups buttermilk
1 egg, beaten
1 teaspoon vanilla extract
½ teaspoon maple flavoring

Combine oatmeal, flour, salt, soda and sugar; mix well. Add oil, buttermilk, egg, vanilla and maple flavoring; mix well. Let stand at room temperature for 30 minutes. Drop a heaping tablespoon of batter on heated, oiled griddle and brown on each side. *Yield: 12 to 15 pancakes. Serve with butter or margarine and syrup.*

Mrs. Raymond Bowers
Clinton County (Plattsburg)

SOMBRERO

2 tablespoons margarine
4 eggs
2 cups milk
2 cups all-purpose flour
Powdered sugar
Lemon juice

Heat oven to 425 degrees. Melt margarine in large square ceramic baking dish in oven. Process eggs in blender at high speed for 15 seconds. Add milk and blend until very frothy. Add flour. Blend about 3 minutes. Tip ceramic baking dish so margarine coats all sides. Pour batter into pan and bake about 20 minutes. Mix powdered sugar and lemon juice to make a thin sauce. Serve sombrero with sauce and fruit. *This is not only delicious for a ladies' luncheon, but my children would happily eat them for breakfast, lunch and supper.*

Mrs. Brian R. Butler (Margaret)
Linn Unit (Brookfield)

SIMPLE CHEESE BAKE

12 slices white bread
½ pound Cheddar cheese
2½ cups milk
4 eggs, beaten
Salt
Freshly ground pepper
Paprika

Remove crusts from bread slices and cut into 1-inch cubes. Shred cheese through large holes of grater. Mix milk and beaten eggs together. Place layer of cubed bread in greased baking dish, followed by a sprinkling of shredded cheese. Continue to layer these ingredients until all are used. Pour egg/milk mixture over all; season with salt and pepper; sprinkle paprika over top. Bake at 350 degrees for about 50 minutes. *Yield: 4 to 6 servings. Recipe can be easily enlarged so it's great for parties. It can also be assembled the day before, refrigerated, and baked to be ready piping hot when you need it. I serve this at a late breakfast on Thanksgiving and Christmas. With fruit and beverage it makes a nice meal. For people with larger appetites I also serve sausage with it.*

Pearl Brooks
Saline County (Marshall)

Variation: Sprinkle with bacon (8 to 10 slices, fried and crumbled), ½ cup sliced fresh mushrooms and ½ cup chopped tomato.
Madeline Wrobley
Jackson County (Kansas City)

Variation: Add 1 pound browned sausage to layers of bread and cheese.
Mrs. Bill L. Trout
Butler County (Poplar Bluff)

Variation: Before baking, add ½ cup milk to 1 can cream of of mushroom soup and pour over casserole. Top with mushrooms slices.
Betty Irvin
Harrison County (Bethany)

EGG CASSEROLE

2 tablespoons butter or margarine
½ cup onion, chopped
2 tablespoons all-purpose flour
1¼ cup milk
1 cup Cheddar cheese, shredded
6 hard-cooked eggs, sliced
1½ cups potato chips, crushed
10 to 12 strips bacon, fried crisp and crumbled

Melt butter. Cook onion in butter until tender. Blend in flour. Cook 1 minute over low heat stirring constantly. Gradually add milk. Cook, stirring constantly, until mixture thickens. Add cheese and simmer until cheese melts completely. In large casserole, layer eggs, then cheese sauce, potato chips, and bacon. Repeat twice. Bake at 350 degrees for 30 minutes. *Yield: 6 servings.*

Vickie Pabst
Callaway County (Holts Summit)

AND JOPLIN WAS ITS NAME

In 1839 a young Methodist preacher from Tennessee selected a site for his log cabin near the edge of the timber not far from today's Fifth and Club Streets in Joplin. The Reverend Harris G. Joplin staked out land by a spring, which came to be known as Joplin's Spring, and the creek into which it flowed was called Joplin Creek. Reverend Joplin's cabin was the meeting house for the district's first worshippers, and those who heard him preach remembered his eloquence and his fine voice. He was excitable, swaying his listeners with the strength of his own feeling. He was not a big man, only five feet eight inches tall, but he seemed big when he began to preach.

After a few years he moved away, leaving no trace of his cabin or of his congregation — but his spring remained, and his name — Joplin Creek. Later when lead was discovered near the bed of this little creek, the mining camp that sprang up around it was known as Joplin Camp. Thus Joplin, once a rip-roaring mining camp, was named for a gentle preacher of the word of God.

Soups and Sandwiches

Soups

CHICKEN GUMBO FILÉ

- 6 tablespoons shortening
- 6 tablespoons flour
- 1 minced onion
- ¼ cup chopped celery
- 1 pound chopped okra
- 1 chicken, cut into serving pieces
- 6 cups water
- 2 tablespoons salt
- 2 teaspoons pepper
- 1 chopped green pepper
- ½ cup parsley
- ½ teaspoon gumbo filé

Heat fat. Add flour, stirring constantly until flour is desired shade of brown. This is a *roux.* Add onion, celery and okra. Stir until vegetables are slightly wilted. Then, add chicken. Add water; mix well to dissolve roux. Add salt and pepper. Cover pot with tight-fitting lid. Cook on low heat for 1½ to 2 hours. Add green pepper and parsley to gumbo 5 minutes before removing from heat. Then add filé. *Do not cook after adding filé. Two dozen oysters may be added 15 minutes before removing from heat for extra flavor.*

Mary Ann Viorel
Marion County (Hannibal)

SPLIT PEA SOUP

- 1 cup dried split peas
- 6 cups water
- 2 chicken bouillon cubes
- 1 cup cooked ham, diced
- ½ cup celery, chopped
- 1 large carrot, chopped
- 1 small onion, chopped
- 1 tablespoon butter or margarine
- 1 teaspoon sugar
- 1 teaspoon salt
- ¼ teaspoon pepper
- ½ teaspoon garlic powder

Place all ingredients in heavy pot. Bring to a boil. Lower heat and simmer, covered, for 2 hours. *May also be cooked in pressure cooker for 30 minutes. Very good.*

Evelyn Crutchfield
Macon Unit (Macon)

POTATO SOUP WITH EGG NOODLES

Soup:

6 medium potatoes, peeled and diced
½ cup chopped onion
Diced carrots, if desired
¼ cup butter
1 pint (2 cups) milk
Salt and pepper to taste

Cover potatoes, onions and carrots with water and simmer until tender. Mash potatoes in liquid with potato masher. Add butter, milk, salt and pepper.

Egg noodles:

2 cups flour
1 egg
1 tablespoon water
½ teaspoon salt
Dash pepper

Make a well in the flour and drop in egg, water, salt and pepper. With a fork, whip egg mixture and mix in flour until too stiff to use fork. Put on a floured board and knead until stiff. Roll out very thin and cut in 2-inch strips. Stack the strips, sprinkling each with flour. With a sharp knife, cut into very narrow strips. Air dry for at least 30 minutes. Drop into boiling potato soup and simmer for 10 to 15 minutes. *Yield: 4 servings. This is a recipe from my mother, Frances Miner, and is really good in cold weather.*

Helen E. Miner
Cape Girardeau County (Cape Girardeau)

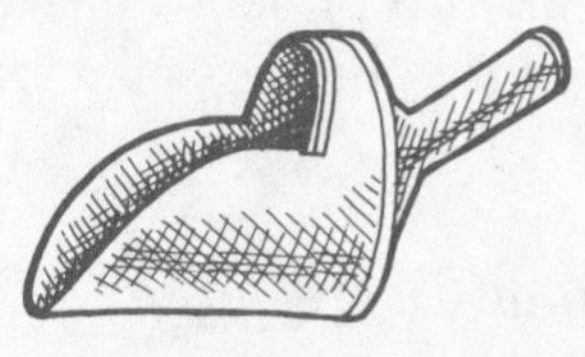

CANADIAN CHEESE SOUP

2 tablespoons chopped onion
2 tablespoons margarine
¼ cup flour
2 cups light cream or ½ milk, ½ evaporated milk
2 cups chicken bouillon or broth
½ pound sharp Cheddar cheese, shredded
½ cup cooked shredded carrots
½ cup cooked diced celery
¼ teaspoon salt
2 tablespoons minced parsley

Sauté onion in margarine. Add flour; mix. Stir in cream and chicken broth. Cook until smooth and thickened. Add cheese, carrots, celery and salt. Heat until cheese is melted. Serve topped with parsley. *Yield: 10 servings. I developed this recipe for our patients at the Independence Sanitarium and Hospital as a way to increase nutrition for patients not eating well.*

Barbara Ann Dudley
Jackson County — Independence Unit (Independence)

Sandwiches

PIMENTO CHEESE SPREAD

2 packages mild Cheddar cheese
1 (4-ounce) jar pimentos
2 pinches salt
¼ cup sugar
¾ to 1 cup salad dressing

Grind cheese and pimentos together. Add remaining ingredients. Refrigerate overnight before using as this will give the cheese a chance to absorb pimento taste. *Note: Very tasty as a sandwich spread and on crackers as a snack.*

Beverly Pickering
Worth County (Grant City)

SATURDAY NIGHT SPECIAL

1 (8-ounce) package cream cheese, softened
2 tablespoons horseradish
¼ cup crumbled bacon
6 slices enriched Russian rye bread
18 ounces thinly sliced smoked turkey
1½ cups shredded cabbage
1 cup shredded carrots
¼ cup minced green onion
⅓ cup oil and vinegar salad dressing

Whip together cream cheese, horseradish and bacon until light and fluffy. Spread cheese mixture evenly on bread; cover with 3 ounces turkey. Combine cabbage, carrots and onion; stir in salad dressing. Top each sandwich with vegetable mixture. Garnish with pitted black olives and cherry tomatoes. *Yield: 6 sandwiches.*

Barbara Ann Dudley
Jackson County — Independence Unit (Independence)

"AS YOU LIKE IT" SANDWICHES

1 (8-ounce) package cream cheese, softened
¼ cup orange or pineapple juice
¼ cup fruit preserves
6 slices enriched raisin bread
1½ cups sliced fresh fruit
¼ cup warmed honey

Beat cream cheese and juice until light and fluffy. Gently stir in preserves. Toast bread and trim crusts, if desired. Spread about ¼ cup cheese mixture on each toast slice. Arrange sliced fruit on top and drizzle with warm honey. Serve open-faced. *Note: Suggested combinations: strawberry preserves and fresh strawberries, orange marmalade and fresh peaches. Garnish with orange twists and mint leaves. Yield: 6 sandwiches.*

Barbara Ann Dudley
Jackson County — Independence Unit (Independence)

Use cookie cutters for cheese and lunchmeat for children's sandwiches at parties.

FOOTBALL SATURDAY SANDWICHES

Cheese Sauce:
- 2 tablespoons butter
- 2 tablespoons flour
- ¼ teaspoon salt
- ⅛ teaspoon pepper
- 1 cup milk
- 1 teaspoon dry mustard
- 1 cup shredded Cheddar cheese
- ½ teaspoon Worcestershire sauce
- 1½ teaspoons cooking sherry
- 1 loaf French bread
- 3 packages thin-sliced sandwich meat

Melt butter in saucepan, stir in flour, salt, and pepper. Cook over low heat until bubbly. Stir in milk; add dry mustard and shredded cheese, Worcestershire and cooking sherry. Heat over low heat, stirring constantly until cheese is melted and sauce is smooth. Cut bread in half lengthwise. Layer meat on bottom half. Cover with cheese sauce. Place other half on top and slice in 1 or 2-inch thick slices. Place in a 9-x-13-inch baking dish. Cover with foil; bake at 300 degrees until heated through, about 25 minutes. *Several of these are great to pop in the oven after a football game. Can be made ahead.*

Sara Barham
Dade County (Greenfield)

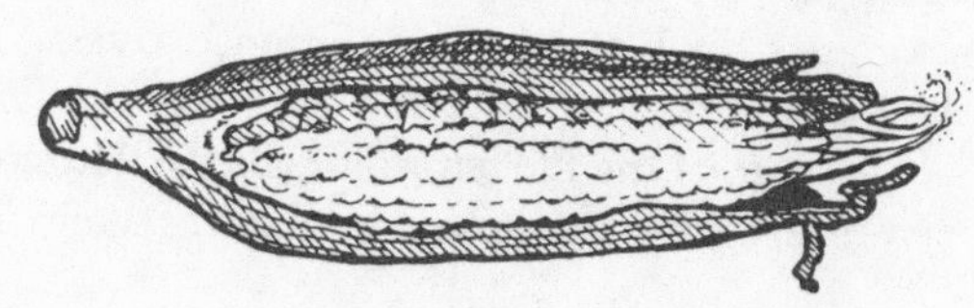

BIG SPRINGS

No other part of Missouri offers such a variety of attractions as the Big Springs region. Through most of the year a carpet of green covers Southeast Missouri. The wooded Ozark hills and valleys include six large sections of the Mark Twain National Forest. With a low population density, this part of the state is especially good for camping, hiking and other forms of outdoor fun.

Winding among the forests and hills are the region's waterways — rivers, lakes and 60 major springs. Big Springs (pictured to the left), 4 miles south of Van Buren, produces up to 846 million gallons of crystal-clear water each day and is the largest single-outlet spring in the nation.

From the springs comes the water for many famed rivers. Two of them, the Current and the Jacks Fork, are protected as part of the Ozark National Scenic Riverways. These, plus the Eleven Point, Black, Huzzah, Big Piney, and St. Frances rivers are among those popular for canoeing and float fishing.

Breads

CHEESE BISCUITS

3 sticks butter or margarine less 1 inch of 1 stick
1 pound sharp Cheddar cheese, shredded
1 pound (2 cups) flour
Salt
Dash of red pepper
Pecan halves

Cream butter and cheese. Add flour, salt and pepper. Mix well. When dough is very smooth, pinch off pieces the size of marbles. Flatten slightly by pressing pecan half on top of each. Bake on ungreased cookie sheet about 12 minutes at 450 degrees.

Lynn Hall
Crawford County

SNOW BISCUITS

1 package dry yeast
¾ cup warm water
2 cups flour
1 teaspoon salt
2 tablespoons sugar
3 tablespoons vegetable oil

Dissolve yeast in warm water; set aside. Sift dry ingredients. Add oil and yeast mixture. Mix well. Pour onto floured board. Knead well. Work in extra flour if needed. Pinch off 12 biscuits. Put in greased pan and let rise 30 to 40 minutes. Bake at 450 degrees for about 18 minutes.

Evelyn Staats
Reynolds County (Ellington)

NEVER FAIL CORN BREAD

2 cups buttermilk
1 teaspoon baking soda
1½ teaspoons salt
2 cups corn meal
1 egg
¼ cup shortening *or* bacon drippings

Add salt and soda to buttermilk. Stir slightly, then add corn meal; stir then add egg. Beat mixture thoroughly. Heat 1 10-inch skillet; add the fat when hot. Be sure bottom of skillet is covered with fat and pour remaining fat in the corn meal mixture. Bake at 450 degrees about 15 to 20 minutes until brown.

Alice Baker
Osage County (Chamois)

RAISIN BRAN MUFFINS

1 (15-ounce) package raisin bran cereal
3½ cups sugar
5 cups flour
5 teaspoons baking soda
2 teaspoons salt
4 beaten eggs
1 cup vegetable oil
1 quart buttermilk

Use extra large mixing bowl. Mix bran, sugar, flour, salt and soda. Add eggs, oil and buttermilk. Mix well. Store in covered container in refrigerator. Use as desired. Batter will keep in refrigerator up to 6 weeks. Fill greased muffin tins ⅔ full. Bake at 400 degrees for 15 to 20 minutes. *Yield: Approximately 5 dozen. Note: Muffins freeze well after baking.*

Mrs. Richard Sullins (Lillian)
Monroe County (Madison)

BEER BREAD

3 cups self-rising flour
3 tablespoons sugar
1 (12-fluid ounce) can of warm beer

Add sugar to flour in a large mixing bowl. Stir in beer until well mixed. Pour batter into a greased 9-x-5-inch loaf pan. With wet hands, smooth top of batter. Bake at 350 degrees for 35 minutes. Remove from oven and butter top generously. Remove from pan and it's ready to slice and serve. *This is quick and easy to make and serve any time you would like a hot yeast bread.*

Harriett Rader
Webster County (Marshfield)

FROZEN CRESCENT ROLLS

2 cups lukewarm milk
2 packages yeast
1 cup sugar
1 cup shortening
2 teaspoons salt
6 eggs, beaten
9 cups flour
½ cup margarine, melted

Scald milk and cool to lukewarm. Add yeast and stir until dissolved. Cream the sugar, shortening and salt. Add the eggs and mix. Add ½ the flour then the milk and yeast mixture and mix. Add remaining flour. Knead on a floured board. Put into a greased large bowl and let rise until doubled in bulk (about 2 hours). Divide the dough into 4 parts. Roll each part into a circle and spread with the melted margarine. Cut into 16 wedge-shaped pieces. Roll each piece, starting at the large end and place on a baking sheet. Freeze immediately. When frozen, place in plastic bags and seal. Store in freezer until ready to use. To bake, place on greased baking sheet. Let rise 3 to 4 hours. Bake at 350 degrees for 12 to 15 minutes. *Makes 64 extra good rolls.*

Mary Jean Voepel
Ralls County (Center)

HOT ROLLS

2 cakes yeast
2 cups lukewarm water, divided
¾ cup sugar
½ cup melted shortening
1½ teaspoons salt
2 eggs
7 cups flour

Soften yeast in ½ cup lukewarm water; set aside. Blend together 1½ cups water, sugar, salt, shortening and cool to lukewarm. Add yeast mixture, well beaten eggs and a small amount of flour at a time. Gradually beat in flour until all is used, cover and let rise until double in bulk. Make out rolls to desired shape and let rise again about 1 hour. Bake at 425 degrees about 20 minutes or until brown. *Makes 4 dozen rolls.*

Kathleen Gardner
Harrison County (New Hampton)

Similar recipe submitted by:
Mrs. Harold E. Woods
Ralls County (Perry)
Variation: Use hot potato water to dissolve sugar, salt and shortening.
Betty Wertz
St. Charles County (St. Charles)

EASY ROLLS

½ cup shortening
1 teaspoon salt
¼ cup sugar
½ cup boiling water
1 package dry yeast
½ cup warm water
1 egg
3 cups flour

In mixing bowl, put shortening, salt and sugar. Pour boiling water over this. Stir until dissolved and cool. Mix yeast with warm water. Add to first mixture. Add egg and beat. Add flour to make a sticky dough. Refrigerate, covered, overnight. Next day take out as much as needed. Roll out and cut with biscuit cutter or pinch out. Dip in melted butter. Let rise 1 to 1½ hours. Bake at 400 degrees for 12 to 15 minutes. *Makes approximately 2 dozen rolls. Given to me by my mother, Mrs. Helen Young of Alton, Missouri.*

Mrs. Roger Garner (Cathy)
Howell County (West Plains)

Variation: For rusk (bread for toasting): combine equal amounts of this dough and bread dough. Shape into loaf and put into greased pan. Let rise in warm place about 1 hour. Bake at 375 degrees for 30 to 40 minutes until brown and bread begins to pull from sides of pan.
Mary Lou McKee
Clark County (Kahoka)

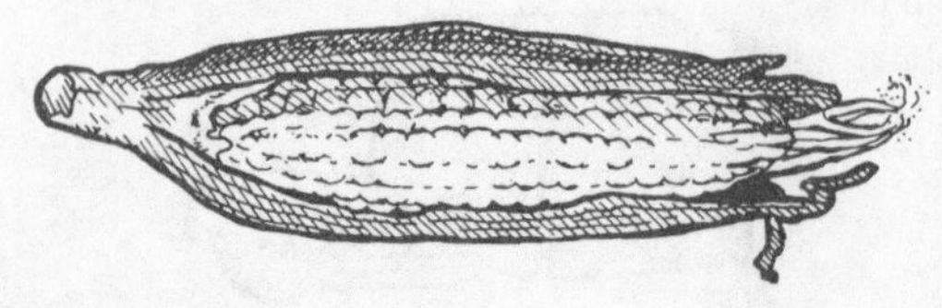

COTTAGE CHEESE YEAST ROLLS

2 packages active dry yeast
½ cup lukewarm water
2 cups small curd cottage cheese
¼ cup sugar
2 eggs
2 teaspoons salt
½ teaspoon baking soda
4½ cups sifted flour

Sprinkle yeast on warm water and stir to dissolve. Heat cottage cheese until lukewarm. Combine cottage cheese, sugar, salt, soda, eggs, yeast and 1 cup flour in a bowl. Beat with an electric mixer until smooth, about 2 minutes, scraping bowl. Gradually add flour to make a soft dough. Place in greased bowl and let rise until doubled in bulk, about 1½ hours. Brush tops of rolls with 1 egg plus 1 tablespoon water. Sprinkle with sesame seeds. Bake at 350 degrees for 20 minutes or until golden brown. *Make large rolls for hamburgers; smaller for parties.*

Mrs. Lorene Sly Maris
Atchison County (Fairfax)

SWEET PETALS

1 package dry yeast or 1 cake compressed yeast
¼ cup warm water
3 tablespoons margarine
2 tablespoons sugar
1 teaspoon salt
¾ cup hot scalded milk
3 cups all-purpose flour

Soften yeast in warm water. In a large mixing bowl, combine margarine, sugar, salt and milk. Cool to lukewarm. Stir in the softened yeast and gradually add flour to form a stiff dough. Knead on floured surface until smooth and satiny, 3 to 5 minutes. Place in greased bowl. Cover, let rise in warm place (85 to 90 degrees) until light and doubled in size, about 1 hour. Pinch off small piece of dough, enough to roll into a 6-inch strip, ½-inch thick. Dip into melted margarine (½ cup) then in cinnamon-sugar topping. Wind into a flat coil in center of pan. Continue making strips placing them close together to make a round flat coffee cake. Sprinkle with leftover sugar mixture. Cover, let rise in warm place until doubled in size, about 1 hour. Bake at 350 degrees for about 25 minutes. Cool slightly. Drizzle with a glaze of ½ cup powdered sugar and 1 to 2 teaspoons milk.

Cinnamon-sugar topping:
¾ cup sugar
¼ cup brown sugar
2 teaspoons cinnamon
¾ cup chopped pecans

This is a delicious coffee cake. I usually triple the recipe and have good results. At Christmas I sprinkle red crystal sugars on top of cake.

Mrs. Melvin George (Crystal)
Chariton County (Salisbury)

ORZECHOWE CIASTKA (WALNUT HORNS)

2 cakes yeast
1 pint sour cream
1 cup shortening
1 cup margarine
1 teaspoon salt
3 eggs, separated
2 teaspoons vanilla extract
5 cups flour
2 cups nuts, chopped
1 cup sugar
Dash cinnamon

Dissolve yeast in sour cream. Set aside. Mix shortening, margarine, salt, egg yolks and vanilla with mixer. Add sour cream mixture slowly. Add flour. You will need to mix by hand. Mixture will form a ball. Put in bowl and cover. Refrigerate overnight. Next day, roll dough on board as for pie pastry. Spread filling over dough. Cut into wedges and roll from large end. Dip in egg whites then in a mixture of nuts, sugar and cinnamon. Bake at 350 degrees for 15 to 20 minutes until brown.

Filling:
Any Solo brand cake, pastry or dessert filling may be used, or strawberry or cherry preserves.

Mrs. Matt Kowalski (Helen)
Buchanan County (St. Joseph)

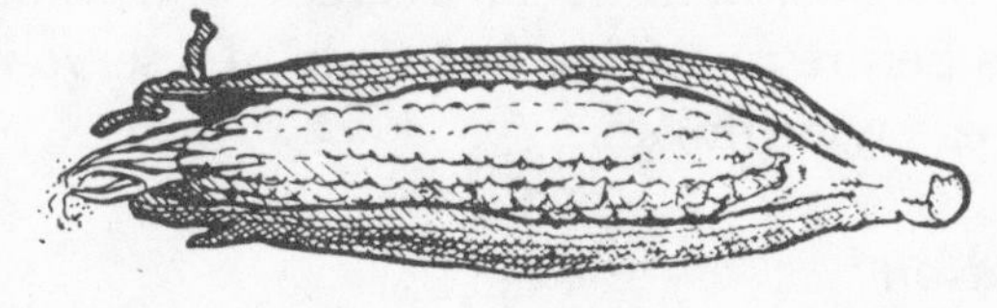

COFFEE CAKE

½ cup margarine
1 cup sugar
2 eggs
2 cups flour
1 teaspoon baking soda
1 teaspoon baking powder
½ teaspoon salt
1 cup sour cream
1 teaspoon vanilla extract

Mix together margarine, sugar and eggs. Add flour, soda, baking powder, and salt. Mix well. Add sour cream and vanilla. Put half of batter in well greased and floured 9-inch square pan. Spread about half the topping mixture over batter. Add remaining batter. Add remaining topping, spreading over top. Bake at 325 degrees for 50 minutes. *Serves 9. Delicious any time.*

Topping:
⅓ cup brown sugar
¼ cup white sugar
1 teaspoon cinnamon
1 cup nuts, optional

Mrs. Nellis G. Christman (Charlotte)
Monroe County (Paris)

Variation: For Monkey Bread: use 3 cans buttermilk biscuits (10 per can), 1 cup sugar, 2 teaspoons cinnamon, 1 cup brown sugar, ½ cup margarine. Cut each biscuit into fourths with scissors. Shake biscuits in a bag with sugar and cinnamon. Layer in a greased tube pan. Sprinkle with nuts between layers, if desired. Mix brown sugar and margarine and boil 1 minute. Pour over biscuits. Bake at 350 degrees for 35 minutes. Let stand 10 minutes before removing from pan. To serve just pinch off a piece and eat with fingers.

Lois Davidson
Worth County (Worth)

FEATHER BED BUNS

1 cake or package yeast
1½ tablespoons sugar
1 cup lukewarm milk
Flour
¼ cup shortening
1 teaspoon salt
1 egg, beaten

Soak yeast and sugar in milk for 10 minutes. Beat in 1 cup flour; add shortening and salt; beat. Add beaten egg. Beat batter, gradually adding more flour to make a stiff dough. Turn onto floured board and knead. Let rise until double in bulk. Punch down, shape into buns. Let rise again until doubled. Bake at 325 degrees for about 25 minutes. *This was my mother's special bun recipe; it's very old. My mother has been gone since 1946.*

Helen B. Thompson
Shannon County (Birch Tree)

Sift dry baking ingredients onto a paper plate. The paper plate bends easily for pouring.

HA HA TONKA STATE PARK

The Ha Ha Tonka water tower is one of two old buildings, ravaged by a 1942 fire, that gave the name to one of Missouri's newest state parks. The 2,274-acre park is located on the Niangua arm of the Lake of the Ozarks, five miles south of Camdenton and contains several caves, a natural bridge and one of Missouri's largest springs. It is open for day use only with picnic sites and hiking trails.

The Ha Ha Tonka area was the home of both the Osage and the Kickapoo Indians and derives its name from a native word meaning "laughing waters." Early American explorers like Zebulon Pike and Daniel Boone trapped and hunted in the area, and its beauty attracted many Missourians. One of these, Kansas Citian Robert Snyder, "discovered" the area in the late 1890s and bought 2,500 acres there. He then imported 20 Scottish stonemasons to cut nearby bluff rock and build a 60-room European-style castle, water tower and guest house overlooking the Niangua River.

Snyder's death left the mansion unfinished until 1922, when the family completed it for a summer home and "hotel" for friends. In 1942, however, it was gutted by fire, leaving only the crumbling stone walls which dominate the scenery.

Salads

ARTICHOKE SALAD

1 package chicken flavored Rice-A-Roni
1 can or jar regular or marinated artichokes, diced
1 bunch green onions, diced
½ stalk celery, diced
1 medium-sized jar green olives, diced
1 cup mayonnaise

Cook Rice-A-Roni as directed on package. Drain liquid from artichokes and reserve. Mix rice, artichokes, onions, celery, and olives together. Mix reserved liquid with mayonnaise; add to mixture. Chill several hours or overnight. Serve cold. *Serves 10 to 12.*

Orene Hubbard
Ozark County (Gainesville)

BEAUTIFUL FRUIT SALAD

1½ cups sugar
¼ cup cornstarch
2 cans fruit cocktail, drained and juice reserved
Sliced bananas
Pineapple chunks
Fresh strawberries or frozen whole strawberries
Any other fruit, if desired

Mix sugar and cornstarch with juice from fruit cocktail. Cook until thick; cool. Add fruit cocktail and all other fruit. *Note: The glaze is clear when cool and lets the fruit retain their natural colors.*

Nancy Summers
Holt County (Maitland)

GAZPACHO SALAD

1 (3-ounce) package lemon gelatin
½ cup boiling water
1 (16-ounce) can stewed tomatoes
1 cup chopped celery
1 cup chopped green pepper

Dissolve gelatin in boiling water. Add remaining ingredients and chill until set. Top each salad serving with topping. Garnish with a sprig of parsley. Serves 12. *Easily served from a 3-quart Pyrex baking dish.*

Optional topping:
½ cup salad dressing or mayonnaise
½ cup sour cream
1 tablespoon lemon juice
1 tablespoon orange juice
2 teaspoons sugar

Mrs. Dan L. Stanley (Melanie)
Jasper County (Joplin)

OLD FASHIONED POTATO SALAD

5 pounds potatoes (small red)
3 or 4 stalks celery
4 hard cooked eggs
3 or 4 small sweet pickles
2 cups mayonnaise
¼ cup pickle juice

Boil potatoes with skins on until tender, but not over cooked. When potatoes are done, pour cold water over them to cool. Peel skin from potatoes and cut into quarters. Dice celery, 3 hard cooked eggs and pickles. Mix potatoes, celery, eggs and pickle together in large bowl. Salt and pepper to taste. Put mayonnaise and pickle juice into salad and stir well. Place in serving bowl and sprinkle with paprika. *Garnish with remaining egg. Yield: 10 or more servings.*

Dennis C. Abel
St. Louis County—Southwest County Unit (Baldwin)

DANDELION POTATO SALAD

1½ cups thinly sliced warm boiled potatoes
1 teaspoon salt
1 tablespoon sugar
2 tablespoons vinegar
2 tablespoons water
2 tablespoons hot bacon fat
3 cups dandelion greens

Mix all ingredients, except greens; then toss lightly with greens. *Note: Only the small young tender dandelion leaves that come up early in the spring should be used. Once the flowers appear, the leaves will be bitter.*

Donna Fisher
St. Charles County (St. Charles)

VERMICELLI SALAD

1 (14-ounce) package coil vermicelli
2 tablespoons vegetable oil
1 cup Italian salad dressing
2 tablespoons parsley, chopped
2 tablespoons chives, chopped
¼ teaspoon dried basil
¼ teaspoon dried oregano
1 to 1¼ cups mayonnaise
2 tablespoons red wine vinegar (or tarragon vinegar)
Seasoned salt to taste
Garlic salt to taste
Coarse ground pepper to taste

Cook vermicelli in large kettle of boiling water with vegetable oil. Add vermicelli gradually to boiling water, so that water doesn't stop boiling. Stir constantly until pasta is limp. Stir frequently until pasta is just tender, about 10 or 12 minutes. Drain immediately. Rinse. Drain again. In large mixing bowl, combine vermicelli with remaining ingredients, mixing thoroughly but gently after each addition. Chill thoroughly, overnight if possible. *Try this instead of potato salad for your next cook-out or picnic!*

Mrs. J. Loren Washburn (Anita)
Morgan County (Versailles)

TACO SALAD

1 head lettuce, shredded
½ pound mild cheese, shredded
1 (15-ounce) can ranch style beans or kidney beans, chilled and drained
2 tomatoes, diced
½ onion, chopped
1 pound ground beef, browned, drained and cooled
1 package taco seasoning
¾ bottle Kraft Catalina Dressing, chilled
1 large package corn chips

Combine all ingredients except Catalina dressing and corn chips. Add these just before serving.

Donna Daniel
Stoddard County (Essex)

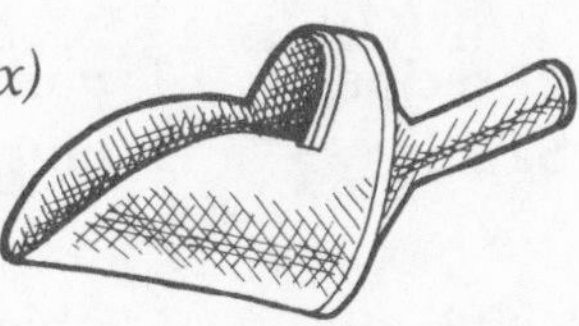

SAUERKRAUT SALAD

1 large can finely chopped sauerkraut, drained
¾ cup chopped green pepper
¾ cup chopped celery
¼ cup chopped onion
½ cup (small can) red pimento
1 cup sugar
¼ cup vinegar

Combine sauerkraut, green pepper, celery, onion and pimento. Bring sugar and vinegar to a boil. Pour over sauerkraut mixture and let stand overnight.

Mrs. Mary Miller
Warren County (Warrenton)

Variation: May use ½ cup shredded carrots instead of pimento.
Mrs. Chester Clark
Clay County — Liberty Unit (Liberty)

LAYERED SALAD

Salad:

1 head iceburg lettuce
1 head endive lettuce
1 head romaine lettuce
1 head escarole
6 hard cooked eggs
½ pound shredded Cheddar cheese
1 large bunch chopped green onions
1 (10-ounce) package frozen peas, uncooked
¼ pound chopped bacon, fried crisp

Chop all 4 heads of lettuce into bite-sized pieces. Slice eggs. Then layer ingredients as listed above into a large bowl.

Dressing:

1 envelope original recipe Hidden Valley Salad Dressing Mix
1 pint Hellman's mayonnaise
1 pint sour cream

Mix the ingredients well; it will be quite thick. Carefully spread the dressing on top of salad, sealing to the edges of the bowl so that the salad is completely covered. Cover and refrigerate 24 hours. Toss just before serving. *This tastes equally good with just plain head lettuce, but the different kinds make it look nice. This was given to me by a telephone installer who said that it will feed a lot of hungry fellows at a carry-in dinner; and it does!*

Nicolette Papanek
Miller County (Eldon)

Variation submitted by:
Chris Ward
Wayne County (Piedmont)

GARDEN SLAW

8 cups shredded cabbage
2 carrots, shredded
1 green pepper, cut into thin strips
½ cup chopped onion
½ cup cold water

Combine vegetables; sprinkle with cold water; chill.

Dressing for Garden Slaw:

1 envelope unflavored gelatin
¼ cup cold water
⅔ cup sugar
⅔ cup vinegar
2 teaspoons celery seed
1½ teaspoons salt
¼ teaspoon black pepper
⅔ cup vegetable oil

Soften gelatin in cold water; set aside. Mix sugar, vinegar, celery seed, salt and pepper in saucepan; bring to a boil. Remove from heat; stir in softened gelatin. Cool until slightly thickened. Beat well. Gradually beat in oil. Drain chilled vegetables. Pour dressing over vegetables and mix lightly. Place slaw in refrigerator until ready to serve. *Yield: 15 to 20 servings. This slaw may be stored in the refrigerator for several days. Toss lightly before serving.*

Mrs. Mayo Anderson (Freda)
Caldwell County (Kingston)

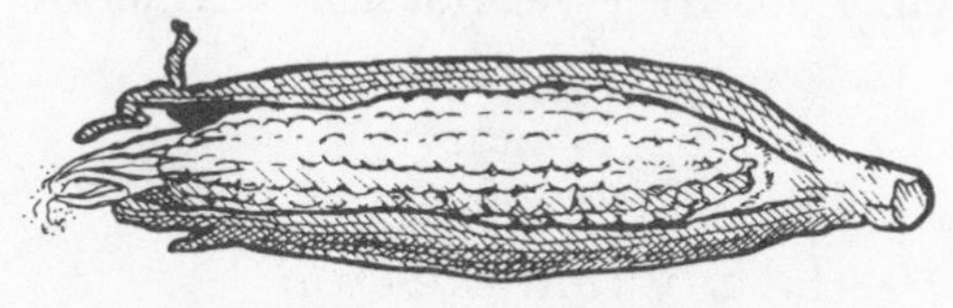

SHRIMP COLE SLAW

1 teaspoon dry mustard
1 teaspoon celery seed
1 tablespoon horseradish
2 heaping tablespoons mayonnaise
3 or 4 ribs celery, finely chopped
1 medium red onion, finely chopped *or* 6 green onions, finely chopped
3 cans small shrimp, well drained

Blend or mash together dry mustard, celery seed and horseradish. Add mayonnaise and mix together. Add celery and onion; mix well. Toss in whole shrimp. This recipe is better if allowed to sit overnight to let flavors blend. Serve with crackers. *I usually double recipe. May be used to stuff tomatoes for salad luncheon.*

Mrs. Paul L. Bradshaw (Susie)
Greene County (Springfield)

CHINESE SLAW

2 (16-ounce) cans chop suey vegetables, drained well
1 (8-ounce) can water chestnuts, sliced and drained
¼ cup slivered almonds
4 to 5 green onions with tops, chopped
½ cup wine vinegar
½ cup sugar
¼ cup vegetable oil
2 teaspoons salt
¼ teaspoon dry mint
½ teaspoon dry mustard
½ teaspoon basil leave
1 teaspoon parsley flakes
1 teaspoon ginger

Mix together the chop suey vegetables, water chestnuts, almonds and green onions. Put remaining ingredients in blender and blend well. Pour over vegetables. Refrigerate overnight or longer.

Mrs. Chester Clark
Clay County — Liberty Unit (Liberty)

VEGETABLE SALAD

- 1 can (16-ounce) French style green beans
- 1 (16-ounce) can whole kernel white corn
- 1 (8-ounce) can small green peas
- 1 (4-ounce) jar pimentoes, diced
- 1 green pepper, diced
- 1 cup celery, diced
- 1 onion, chopped
- 1 teaspoon salt
- Pepper to taste

Mix all ingredients together well. Toss with sauce.

Sauce:

- 1 cup sugar
- ½ cup oil
- ¾ cup vinegar

Mix all together in sauce pan and bring to a boil; boil 3 minutes. Let cool and then pour over vegetables. Chill at least 2 hours before serving.

Hazel Seabaugh
Cape Girardeau County (Cape Girardeau)
Similar recipe submitted by:
Mrs. Nelson Lumson (Leola)
New Madrid County (Catron)

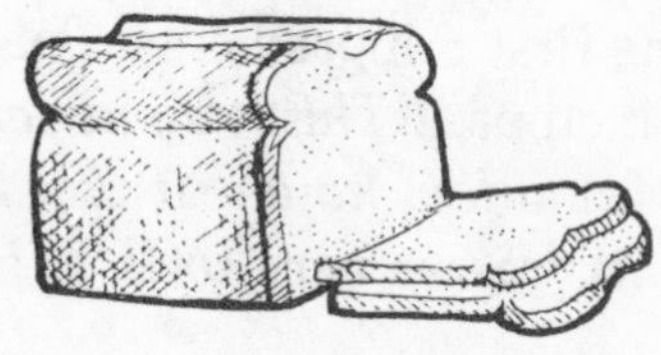

COPPER PENNIES (CARROT SALAD)

2 pounds carrots, thinly sliced
1 teaspoon salt
7 or 8 green onions, with tops, sliced
½ large green sweet pepper, sliced
1 (11-ounce) can tomato soup, undiluted
½ cup vegetable oil
½ cup vinegar
½ cup sugar

Boil carrots in salted water for 4 minutes. They should seem not quite tender if pricked with a fork. Drain carrots. Add onions and green pepper. Heat soup, oil, vinegar, and sugar until it boils. Pour over vegetables and stir lightly. *This recipe makes about 4 cups. It will keep refrigerated for 4 weeks and is nice to have ready to serve anytime.*

Mrs. Earl Baumgardner
Butler County (Poplar Bluff)

QUICK CHERRY SALAD

1 can cherry pie filling
1 can (12-13 ounce) crushed pineapple
¼ cup lemon juice
1 can sweetened condensed milk
2 teaspoons almond extract
1 carton Cool Whip

Thoroughly mix the first 5 ingredients. Fold in the Cool Whip. Spread in a 13-x-9-inch pan. *This may be served at once but it is better refrigerated for a few hours. It will keep several days in the refrigerator. This freezes very well. If frozen, thaw slightly before serving.*

Mrs. Max Foster (Dorothy)
Grundy County (Laredo)

OVERNIGHT VEGETABLE SALAD

1 (10-ounce) package frozen green peas, thawed
1 (16-ounce) can red kidney beans, drained
1 (16-ounce) can cut green beans, drained
1 (12-ounce) can white whole kernel corn, drained
1 cup celery, finely chopped
1 medium onion, chopped
½ cup green pepper, chopped
1 (2-ounce) jar pimento, chopped
¾ cup white vinegar
½ cup sugar
2 tablespoons vegetable oil
1½ teaspoons salt
2 teaspoons water
½ teaspoon paprika

Combine all vegetables and pimento in large bowl. Combine remaining ingredients in small mixing bowl. Stir until sugar is dissolved. Pour over vegetables and toss to mix thoroughly. Refrigerate, covered, at least 24 hours, stirring occasionally. Yield: 14 to 16 servings.

Miss Betty Radcliffe
Stone County North (Crane)

CIRCUS PEANUT SALAD

2 cans crushed pineapple
Water
30 orange Circus Peanuts candy
¼ cup tapioca
1 carton whipped topping

Drain crushed pineapple, reserving juice and add water to juice to make 2 cups. Add candy and tapioca and cook until peanuts melt. Cool. Add whipped topping and pineapple. Chill.

Atholene Cook
Putnam County (Unionville)

BANANA SALAD

2 cups sugar
2 tablespoons flour
2 eggs, beaten
1 cup unsweetened pineapple juice
2 teaspoons lemon juice
1 cup marshmallows
2 tablespoons butter
1 pint (2 cups) whipping cream
6 bananas
1 cup chopped cocktail peanuts

Mix sugar and flour together; add eggs, pineapple and lemon juices. Cook until thick; remove from heat and add marshmallows and butter. Set aside until cool. Whip cream and add to cooled mixture. Alternate this mixture with the bananas and chopped peanuts. Chill until ready to serve.

Mrs. Loy Hollingsworth
Monroe County (Paris)

TANGERINE NUT TOSS

Salad:
1 head lettuce, torn into bite size pieces
2 cups tangerine slices (membrane removed) or mandarin orange sections
½ mild white onion, sliced and separated into rings
¼ cup walnut or pecan croutons (recipe below)

Lightly toss lettuce, oranges and onion rings with dressing. Top with croutons.

Dressing:
⅔ cup sugar
2 teaspoons dry mustard
2 teaspoons salt
1 cup vinegar
1 cup vegetable oil

Mix all ingredients together in a jar; shake well.

Tangerine Nut Toss (continued)

Croutons:
½ cup walnut or pecan halves **¼ teaspoon salt**

Toast pecan or walnut halves mixed with ¼ teaspoon salt.

Maxine Bequette
St. Francois County (Farmington)

TWELVE HOUR SALAD

2 packages lemon flavored gelatin
2 cups hot water
2 cups cold water
2 bananas
1 (16-ounce) can pineapple niblets, drained and juice reserved
8 marshmallows, cut into pieces

Combine all ingredients and chill.

Custard topping:
1 egg
½ cup sugar
2 tablespoons flour
2 tablespoons butter
1 cup pineapple juice

Mix all ingredients together for topping. Cool.

1 cup whipped cream
Shredded cheese

Fold whipped cream into cooled custard. Spread this mixture over the firm gelatin mixture. Let stand 12 hours. Cut into squares and sprinkle with cheese before serving.

Mary Wildman
Wayne County (Piedmont)

FROSTY CRANBERRY FREEZE SALAD

1 (16-ounce) can whole cranberry sauce
1 (8-ounce) can crushed pineapple, drained
1 cup sour cream
1 scant cup pecans, chopped, divided

Combine cranberry sauce, pineapple, sour cream and ⅓ cup chopped pecans. Mix well. Pour into 9-inch square shallow glass baking dish. Freeze until firm, at least 2 hours. Cut into squares to serve. Garnish with remaining ½ cup pecans. *Yield: 9 servings.*

Mrs. J. Clyde Hesselmann (Lynn)
Gasconade County — Gasconade South Unit

FROZEN CRANBERRY SALAD

1 can whole cranberry sauce
1 (20-ounce) can crushed pineapple
1 (11-ounce) can mandarin oranges, drained and cut up
2 cups miniature marshmallows
1 (8-ounce) container sour cream or whipped topping
½ cup powdered sugar
½ cup nuts

Combine the first 4 ingredients then add the sour cream, powdered sugar and nuts. Pour into a 13-x-9-inch pan. Freeze. Set out approximately 30 minutes before serving.

Geraldine Cook
Peggy Miller
Worth County (Allendale)

APRICOT PINEAPPLE SALAD

1 (28-ounce) can apricot halves
1 (28-ounce) can crushed pineapple
1 (3-ounce) package lemon flavored gelatin
1 (3-ounce) package orange flavored gelatin
2 cups boiling water
1 cup apricot and pineapple juices, combined
¾ cup miniature marshmallows

Drain apricots and pineapple and reserve juices. Cut up apricots. Dissolve gelatin in boiling water and add 1 cup combined juices. Chill until almost set and add fruit and marshmallows. Pour into a 9-x-13-inch pan.

Topping:

½ cup sugar
3 tablespoons flour
1 egg, slightly beaten
1 cup combined juices
1 cup whipped cream
2 tablespoons butter
¼ cup shredded cheese

Combine sugar and flour in a saucepan. Blend in egg. Stir in combined juices and cook over low heat, stirring constantly until thick. Remove from heat and stir in butter. Cool and fold in whipped cream. Spread over gelatin and sprinkle with cheese. Chill. *Note: Substitute Dream or Cool Whip for whipped cream if desired. This is very good, and I especially like it with our Thanksgiving or Christmas turkey dinner.*

Mrs. Gerald W. McKenzie
Lafayette County (Oak Grove)

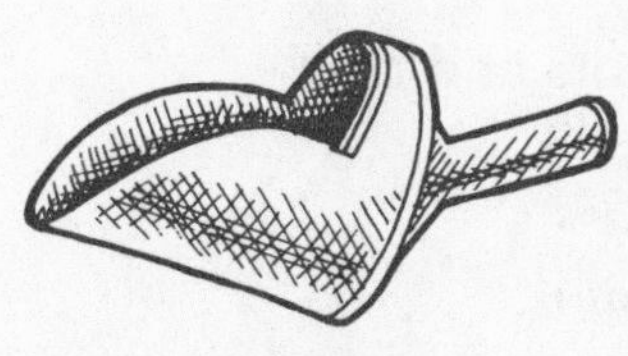

PINEAPPLE CHEESE SALAD

1 pound American cheese, shredded
1 (20-ounce) can crushed pineapple, drained and juice reserved
Equal amount of water as pineapple juice
⅔ cup sugar
2 tablespoons flour
2 eggs, beaten
Pinch of salt
1 tablespoon vinegar

Shred cheese and return to refrigerator while sauce is being cooked. Drain pineapple juice into heavy saucepan, and add equal amount of water. Bring juice and water to a boil. Add flour and sugar that has been mixed well. Add a little hot mixture to beaten eggs. Stir into remaining hot mixture. Add salt and vinegar and cook until thick. Cool. Alternate layers of cheese and pineapple in dish. Spread each layer with sauce. Top layer should be cheese. Refrigerate overnight.

Mrs. Bob McSpadden (Dixie)
Carter County (Van Buren)

APRICOT COTTAGE CHEESE SALAD

1 small carton cottage cheese
1 (3-ounce) package apricot flavored gelatin
1 can white grapes, drained
1 large can crushed pineapple, drained
Pecans, if desired
1 medium container whipped topping

Combine all ingredients and chill.

Anna Louise Snodgrass
Maries County (Vienna)

ORANGE PUDDING SALAD

- 2 packages vanilla tapioca pudding
- 1 package orange flavored gelatin
- 3 cups water
- 1 cup miniature marshmallows
- 1 small can crushed pineapple, undrained
- 1 can mandarin oranges, drained
- 1 small container whipped topping

Combine pudding, gelatin and water; stir. Bring to a boil and continue cooking until thickened. Stir in marshmallows. Let dissolve and cool, about 2 hours at room temperature. Add pineapple and mandarin oranges. Fold in whipped topping. Place in a 13-x-9-inch pan. Refrigerate.

Darlene Thompson
Texas County (Cabool)

PINEAPPLE APRICOT SALAD

- 1 large can crushed pineapple
- 2 packages apricot flavored gelatin
- 2 cups miniature marshmallows
- 1 jar junior size apricot baby food
- 1 (8-ounce) package cream cheese
- 2 cups whipped topping

Heat ½ can pineapple. Add gelatin and marshmallows, stirring constantly until they are dissolved. Add remaining pineapple. Chill until slightly set. Mix the apricots and cream cheese. Combine with gelatin mixture. Stir in the whipped topping and refrigerate for 8 to 12 hours. *This is good with meat dishes, especially pork, or it can be used as a dessert.*

Ervie Meares
McDonald County (Noel)

PINEAPPLE VELVET SALAD

1 (3-ounce) package orange flavored gelatin
10 large marshmallows
1 (8-ounce) package cream cheese, softened
1 cup boiling water
1 package Dream Whip, whipped
½ cup mayonnaise, beaten
1 tall can crushed pineapple
1 cup grated carrots

Combine orange gelatin, marshmallows, cream cheese and boiling water. Stir until all is melted or put in blender to blend well. Chill until gelatin begins to set. Add whipped Dream Whip and mayonnaise. Add crushed pineapple and carrots. Pour into a 9-x-7-inch rectangular or 8-inch square pan. Chill until firm. *Note: Carrots may be grated in blender to give a finer texture. To stretch your servings, add 2 packages gelatin.*

Dorothy Finn
Dent County (Salem)

Variation: For Over The Top Salad: use 2 packages lime gelatin, 1 package lemon gelatin, 3½ cups hot water, ⅔ packages cream cheese, 1 (20-ounce) can crushed pineapple, 1 cup whipped topping. Combine all ingredients as above except whipped topping. Chill until almost set and beat in topping with mixer. Chill.

Mary Wildman
Wayne County (Piedmont)

SPRING HOLIDAY SALAD

1 (3-ounce) package lemon gelatin
1¼ cups boiling water
1 teaspoon prepared mustard
½ teaspoon paprika
½ teaspoon seasoned salt
6 drops yellow food coloring
½ cup finely chopped celery
¼ cup finely sliced green onion
¼ cup finely chopped green pepper
1¼ cups cottage cheese
½ cup heavy cream, whipped
¼ cup sour cream

In a medium bowl, pour boiling water over gelatin; stir until dissolved. Stir in mustard, paprika, seasoned salt and food coloring. Chill until partially set. Fold in celery, onion, and green pepper. Combine cottage cheese, whipped cream or sour cream. Fold into gelatin mixture. Turn into a 4½ cup mold. Chill until firm. Unmold onto greens to serve; garnish with sliced green onions and cherry tomatoes. *Yield: 8 servings.*

Mrs. Allen L. Long (Louise)
Harrison County (Bethany)

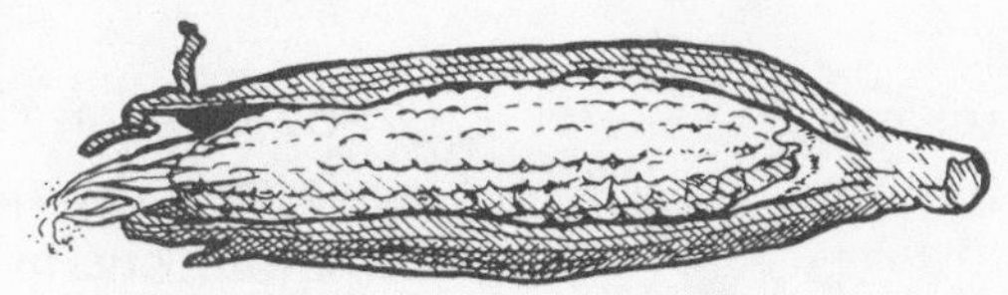

BLUEBERRY GELATIN SALAD

- 2 (3-ounce) packages grape flavored gelatin
- 2 cups boiling water
- 1 cup sweetened crushed pineapple, drained
- 1 (16-ounce) can blueberry pie filling

In a large bowl dissolve gelatin in boiling water. Stir in crushed pineapple and pie filling. Chill until thickened. Spread with topping. *Yield: 8 to 10 servings.*

Topping:

- 1 (8-ounce) carton sour cream
- 1 (8-ounce) package cream cheese
- ⅓ cup sugar
- 1 teaspoon vanilla extract
- ¼ cup crushed nuts

Combine all ingredients except nuts. Spread on gelatin and sprinkle with nuts.

Adbel McCullough
Montgomery County (New Florence)

SINFUL SALAD

- 1 (6-ounce) package strawberry flavored gelatin
- 1 cup boiling water
- 3 medium bananas, mashed
- 1 cup pecans, chopped
- 2 (10-ounce) packages frozen strawberries, partially thawed and drained
- 1 (20-ounce) can crushed pineapple, drained
- 2 cups sour cream

Sinful Salad (continued)

Combine gelatin and boiling water. Stir until gelatin dissolves. Cool. Add mashed bananas, pecans, strawberries and pineapple. Mix well. Pour ½ gelatin mixture into 12-x-8-inch pan. Refrigerate until set, about 1 hour. Spread sour cream evenly over firm gelatin. Cover with remaining, room-temperature, gelatin. Chill at least 2 hours, preferably overnight. *Yield: 12 servings.*

Mary Harris
Christian County (Ozark)

AUNT OPAL'S STRAWBERRY SALAD

2 (10-ounce) packages frozen strawberries, thawed
1 (11¼-ounce) can crushed pineapple, drained, reserve juice
2 (6-ounce) packages strawberry flavored gelatin
3 ripe bananas, mashed
1 (16-ounce) carton sour cream
Whipped cream
Whole strawberries

Combine the juice from the frozen strawberries and canned pineapple with enough hot water to make 3½ cups. Mix with drained fruit, gelatin and bananas. Blend well. Pour ½ mixture into 13-x-9-inch baking dish. Chill until firm. Spread sour cream over gelatin layer. Pour remaining unchilled gelatin over sour cream layer. Chill until firm. To serve, cut into squares, garnish with whipped cream and whole strawberry. *Yield: 18 servings.*

Mrs. B. E. Taylor (Opal)
North Clay Unit (Mystery City)

CLEARWATER LAKE

Clearwater Lake, located on the Black River offers Missourians a spot for recreation and relaxation. Six miles west of Piedmont, Missouri, in Wayne County, the lake has a surface area of 1,630 acres and a shoreline 27 miles long.

Six public recreation areas surrounding the lake provide camping, picnicking and fishing facilities. Squirrel, raccoon, opossum, deer, and turkey thrive in the woods off the lakeshore, and in-season hunting is permitted.

Main Dishes

BARBECUED COON

1 coon, dressed
1 medium onion
2 pods red pepper
Salt to taste
3 stalks celery
1 apple, quartered
1 (2-x-3-inch) piece salt pork
1 tablespoon bacon drippings
Juice of 3 lemons
4 tablespoons margarine, melted
4 to 6 strips bacon

Parboil coon 20 minutes. Drain. Cover with fresh water. Add onion, red pepper, salt, celery, apple, salt pork and bacon drippings. Cook over low heat until coon is tender. Remove meat from bones and chop meat into bite-sized pieces. Place meat in baking dish. Combine your favorite barbecue sauce with lemon juice and margarine. Pour over coon. Bake at 350 until dry and brown.

Mrs. Chip Lewis
Pemiscot County (Hayti)

SMOTHERED QUAIL OR DOVES

8 to 10 doves, quail breasts or whole quail
Flour
Salt and pepper to taste
Dried thyme to taste
Bacon grease
1 (10½-ounce) can beef consomme
1 (10¾-ounce) can cream of mushroom soup
1 (10¾-ounce) can cream of onion soup
⅓ cup sherry
1 teaspoon Beau Monde seasoning
Dash of Worcestershire sauce
2 whole jalapeno peppers

Dust birds with flour. Season with salt, pepper and thyme. Sauté in bacon grease until brown on all sides. Remove birds from pan. Combine remaining ingredients in deep baking dish or roasting pan. Mix well. Add birds. Bake, covered, at 350 degrees for 2 hours. Add water if gravy becomes too thick.

Sammie Martin
Douglas County (Ava)

To hide cooking odors from fish, etc. boil a few cloves, a stick of cinnamon and some peel from a lemon or orange in a small saucepan until the odors are gone.

CHRISTOPHER'S DUCKS

Ducks (allow 1 whole duck for each man; ½ duck for each woman)
Salt to taste
Pieces of raw apple, onion, celery and orange sections

Salt and stuff cavities of ducks with fruit and vegetables. Place ducks in large roasting pan, breast side up, and dot with butter. Brown in hot oven at 400 degrees, then reduce heat to 325 degrees. Lightly cover with basting sauce, cover, and cook 4 or more hours, basting every ½ hour to 45 minutes.

Basting sauce:
1 cup orange marmalade
1 cup cooking sherry
½ cup butter

Warm ingredients in small saucepan. Discard stuffing vegetables before serving. Place ducks on warm platter and serve.

Mrs. Chris Nattinger (Barbara)
Greene County (Springfield)

CHINESE POT ROAST DUCK

4 pound duck with giblets
½ cup soy sauce
1 cup pearl barley
Hot water
½ cup dried mushrooms
3 cups chicken broth
4 slices bacon, chopped
1 medium onion, chopped
1 (3-ounce) can water chestnuts, drained and sliced
2 tablespoons sherry
2 tablespoons soy sauce
Salt
2 tablespoons vegetable oil
Cooked cabbage (recipe follows)

Chinese Pot Roast Duck (continued)

Remove giblets and neck from duck and reserve, place duck in a large pan. Pour the ½ cup soy sauce over duck and let stand at room temperature for about 1½ hours, turning occasionally. Cover barley with hot water and let stand 1 hour. Cover dried mushrooms with hot water and let stand 1 hour. Drain barley and rinse well with cold water; drain again. Bring chicken broth to a boil, add barley and duck neck, cover and simmer for about 30 minutes or until liquid is absorbed and barley is tender, stir occasionally. Discard duck neck. In a wide frying pan, cook bacon partially, add onion and sliced giblets and continue cooking until onion is soft. Rinse and drain mushrooms, chop and mix with onions, add water chestnuts, sherry and the 2 tablespoons soy sauce. Cook a few minutes more, add barley. Salt to taste. Lift duck from soy sauce marinade. Fill breast and body cavity lightly with barley stuffing. Sew the cavities shut with heavy thread. Reserve any extra stuffing and reheat to serve with duck. In a large heavy pan, deep enough to cover duck, heat the oil. Add duck and brown on all sides. Add 1 cup water, cover, and simmer slowly for 1½ hours or until duck is very tender. Place duck on a bed of cooked cabbage on a serving dish. Skim fat from drippings. Cut duck with poultry shears or carve. Spoon some of the drippings over each serving of duck, stuffing, and cabbage.

Cooked cabbage: immerse 6 cups shredded white cabbage in 6 cups boiling, salted water. Drain cabbage as soon as water boils again. Season with 3 tablespoons melted butter, salt and pepper.

Mrs. Lum Young (Marjorie)
Gentry County (Albany)

Beef

TOURNEDOS OF BEEF

½ cup butter, divided
4 pounds beef sirloin tip (or tenderloin), sliced ½-inch thick
2 (6-ounce) cans button mushrooms
2 tablespoons Wilson's B-V sauce
1 tablespoon flour
2 ounces pale dry sherry

Melt 2 tablespoons butter in a large skillet and sauté beef, a few slices at a time, for about 5 minutes or until done. Remove meat from pan and place on a heated platter. Add butter to the pan as needed to continue cooking remaining meat. Set meat aside. Drain mushrooms, reserving the liquid. Add the mushrooms to the pan juices and sauté 2 minutes. Add B-V sauce and stir. To the reserved mushroom liquid add the flour, mix well, and add to the pan juices. Cook, stirring constantly, until creamy. Salt to taste. Add sherry and pour over meat. Serve immediately. *Serves 8. This is a delicious dish for a small dinner party. I like to serve it with wild rice, chilled pears that have been drained and then marinated for 1 to 2 hours in red wine, a spinach salad and hot, crusty French bread.*

Sallie Mogerman
Lincoln County (Troy)

SUKI'S FRIED RICE

- **¾ pound beef chuck steak, partially frozen**
- **6 tablespoons vegetable oil or margarine, divided**
- **1 large onion, peeled, halved and sliced ¼-inch thick**
- **½ small head cabbage, shredded (about 3 cups)**
- **2 large carrots, peeled and coarsely grated, about 1¼ cups**
- **3 cups cooked rice**
- **3 large eggs, beaten**
- **1/8 teaspoon ground black pepper**
- **⅓ to ½ cup soy sauce**
- **6 scallions or green onions, sliced**

Slice beef across the grain into 1/8 inch slices; then cut into ¼-inch slivers. In a 10 to 12 inch skillet or wok, heat 2 tablespoons oil over moderately high heat. Add meat and cook about 3 minutes, stirring constantly. Remove with a slotted spoon. Add 2 tablespoons remaining oil to skillet. Add vegetables and cook 5 to 7 minutes, stirring constantly, until tender; remove with slotted spoon. Add remaining oil to skillet. Add rice and stir until heated about 2 minutes. Reduce heat to moderate and make a large well in the center of the rice. Pour eggs into well; let cook 1 to 2 minutes; without stirring. When eggs are soft set, cut into pieces and mix into rice. Add meat and vegetables, sprinkle with pepper and ⅓ cup soy sauce and stir into rice. Taste and add more soy sauce if desired. Scatter scallions over the top and serve. *Makes 6 to 7 cups.*

Janet Nixon
Clark County (Kahoka)

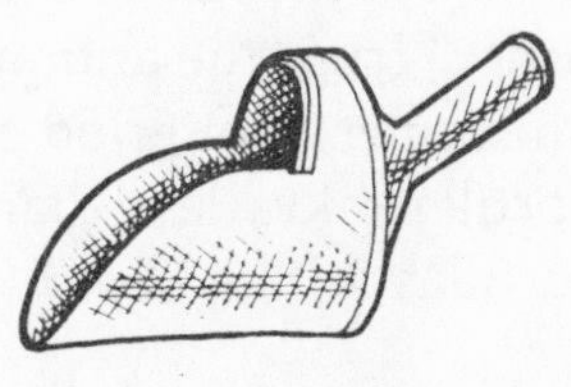

OLÉ ENCHILADAS

2 pounds ground beef (if you desire beef enchiladas)
Salt to taste
1 (8-ounce) jar hot taco sauce
¼ to ½ cup water
½ large can chili powder
3 to 4 cups grated cheese (Velveeta is a favorite)
1½ cups minced onion

Brown ground beef; drain and salt to taste. Add taco sauce and water. (If mixture is too runny, add flour.) Simmer for 20 minutes or until sauce cooks into meat. In a saucepan, mix chili powder and a little water. Mixture should be thin but not too watered down. Bring to a boil, then let cool 5 to 10 minutes. Grease a skillet and place on medium to high heat. Dip tortillas (recipe below) 1 at a time into cooled chili powder mixture. Then heat tortilla in skillet (enough to cook chili powder mixture in.) The tortillas should be orange-red in color, not too pale. The darker the color, the hotter the enchilada. Fill tortilla with beef, cheese and onion. Roll and place in an oblong baking dish. Heat in oven at 350 degrees for 10 minutes. Serve hot. *Warning: This recipe may be hazardous to your kitchen but it's really worth the mess. For Sunday enchiladas substitute boiled hot dogs sliced into bite-sized pieces for the ground beef. Follow the above recipe.*

Flour tortillas:

4 cups flour (not self-rising)
4 teaspoons baking powder
2 teaspoons salt
1 to 1½ cups lukewarm water

Mix dry ingredients. Add water gradually to make a stiff dough. Knead. Pinch dough into balls about 1½ inches in diameter. The dough should yield between 12 to 15 balls. Cover with a dish towel to prevent drying. With a rolling pin, roll each ball into a *very* thin circle (about the size of a saucer). Place on a rod iron hot plate (a "burner" from the antique rod iron stoves our forefathers cooked on) or *very* hot griddle. Turn over when the top bubbles. Each tortilla takes less than 2 minutes to cook. Cover the finished tortillas with a dish towel. This keeps them

Olé Enchiladas (continued)

warm and moist. *Note: To obtain the desired heat for the rod iron hot plate, place on a burner set on high. When you are ready to cook the tortillas, turn the heat down to medium high.*

Kathie Hernandez
Buchanan County (St. Joseph)

BOEUF BURGUNDY

1 small onion, cut into ½-inch wedges
2 cloves garlic, pressed or ⅛ teaspoon garlic powder
2 tablespoons butter or margarine
1 pound lean beef, cut into finger size strips
1 tablespoon flour
½ pound fresh button mushrooms, if large, cut in quarters
½ cup burgundy
1 cup water
½ cup catsup
2 teaspoons salt
½ teaspoon black pepper

Sauté onions and garlic in butter or margarine until onions are clear. Remove from pan. Dredge beef with flour and brown in saucepan. Add mushrooms when meat is half browned. Add sautéed onions. Mix wine, water and catsup and pour over all. Add salt and pepper. Simmer in an oven at 300 degrees or over low heat until meat is tender, 1 to 1½ hours. *Add extra water if it evaporates during cooking. Serve over savory rice, saffron rice or buttered noodles. Serves 4.*

Miss Hulling's Cafeterias
St. Louis County — Central Metro Unit (St. Louis)

STIR FRIED BEEF WITH OYSTER SAUCE

8 ounces flank steak or beef tenderloin
6 green onions, cut into 1-inch pieces
6 ginger roots, sliced
3 cups vegetable oil
1½ tablespoons soy sauce
2½ teaspoons wine (dry sherry)
¼ teaspoon baking soda
6½ tablespoons water
3 teaspoons cornstarch, divided
1 tablespoon oyster sauce
¼ teaspoon sugar
¼ teaspoon black pepper
¼ teaspoon sesame oil

Remove any fat or tough membrane from beef; cut across grain into bite-sized pieces. Mix with 1 tablespoon soy sauce, 1 teaspoon wine, soda, 5 tablespoons water and 2 teaspoons cornstarch. Let soak 1 hour; add ½ tablespoon oil and mix. Heat 3 cups oil for deep frying. Deep fry meat slices over medium heat for 20 seconds until color changes; remove and drain. Remove all but 2 tablespoons oil from pan and reheat. Stir fry green onion and ginger root until fragrant; add beef slices, 1½ teaspoons wine and ½ tablespoon soy sauce, oyster sauce, sugar, pepper, sesame oil, 1½ tablespoons water and 1 teaspoon cornstarch. Toss lightly to mix ingredients and remove to serving plate; serve. Garnish with coriander. *Note: The ½ tablespoon oil added to beef slices prevents slices from sticking together during deep frying.*

Mrs. Pin H. Pu (Elise)
Dunklin County (Kennett)

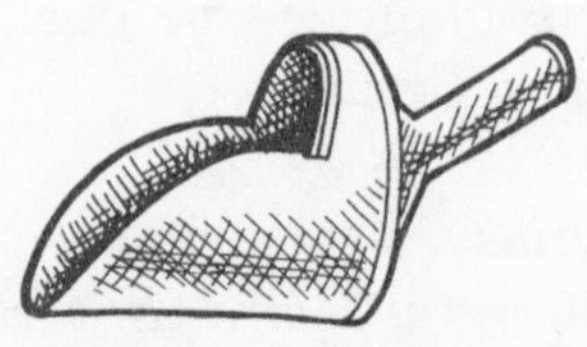

ITALIAN BEEF

- 5 pounds roast beef
- 3 large onions, chopped
- 1 tablespoon salt
- 1½ cups water
- 1 teaspoon garlic salt
- 1 teaspoon oregano
- ½ teaspoon basil
- 1 teaspoon Italian seasoning
- 2 teaspoons MSG
- 3 hot peppers

Combine roast, onions, salt and water. Cover and bake at 325 degrees for 2 hours or until tender. Remove roast to cool. Slice thin. To liquid in roaster, add rest of seasonings; bring to a boil and add peppers. Add cut meat to this liquid, cover and refrigerate for 24 hours. To serve, warm at 350 degrees for 30 minutes. *Use hard rolls; cut and place liquid from meat on each piece of roll and then top with meat. The more you heat the better it gets. This recipe has been enjoyed by our family and friends. It goes a long way when having a group. It's great when we have company for the weekend. You prepare it a day ahead and pop it in the oven 30 minutes before serving.*

Mrs. Leon Craig (Linda)
Livingston County (Chillicothe)

DUTCH OVEN STEAK AND VEGETABLES

2 pounds round steak
Seasoned flour
Vegetable oil
2 potatoes, peeled and halved
4 carrots, peeled and cut in 1-inch chunks
2 small onions, quartered
2 celery stalks, cut in 1-inch chunks
Salt and pepper

Dredge steak in seasoned flour and brown quickly in small amount of oil in a Dutch oven. Set aside. Put flat rack in bottom of Dutch oven. Arrange vegetables on top of rack. Season with salt and pepper to taste. Add water to top of rack. Put steak on top of vegetables. Cover and cook at 350 degrees for 1 hour. Juice can be thickened for gravy. *Yield: 2 to 4 servings. Pearl Miner, my New York grandmother, taught my mother how to prepare this, and it has been a family favorite.*

Helen E. Miner
Cape Girardeau County (Cape Girardeau)

When making bread crumbs in a food processor, process a piece of lemon zest with the bread and use to garnish fish dishes or as casserole toppings.

BAKED BEEF BRISKET

4 pounds beef brisket
2 teaspoons salt
½ teaspoon pepper
1 clove garlic, minced
3 medium onions, thickly sliced
2 tablespoons cornstarch, dissolved in 1 cup cold water

Place brisket in 13-x-10-inch shallow pan, fat side up. Season with salt and pepper. Sprinkle garlic on top of roast and cover with onion slices. Bake at 350 degrees, uncovered, for 1 hour or until onions brown. Add 1 cup hot water, cover with aluminum foil and seal tightly. Reduce heat to 300 degrees. Bake 2 more hours. Transfer meat to serving platter. In pan, thicken juices with cornstarch dissolved in water. Cook and stir until thick and boiling. Serve with brisket. *Yield: 12 servings.*

Mary Kay Lyle
Andrew County (Savannah)

PEPPER STEAK

1 large round steak
1 tablespoon paprika
2 tablespoons butter
2 crushed cloves garlic
1½ cups beef broth
1 cup sliced green onion
2 green peppers, cut into strips
2 tablespoons cornstarch
¼ cup water
¼ cup soy sauce
2 large tomatoes, cut up

Pound steak until ¼-inch thick. Cut into strips. Sprinkle with paprika and let stand. Use large skillet, brown in the butter, add garlic and beef broth. Cover and simmer 30 minutes. Stir in green onions and green peppers. Cover. Cook 5 minutes more. Blend cornstarch, water and soy sauce. Stir into meat mixture until thickened, about 2 minutes. Add tomatoes and stir gently. Serve over rice.

Bernice James
Maries County (Vichy)

Ground Beef

SPAGHETTI SAUCE

½ pound chopped bacon
2½ pounds ground beef
2 cups onion, finely chopped
1 cup green pepper, chopped
6 garlic cloves, chopped
3 (35-ounce) cans Italian plum tomatoes or 35 ounces home canned tomatoes
3 (6-ounce) cans tomato paste
1½ cups dry red wine, divided
5 teaspoons oregano, divided
5 teaspoons basil, divided
1½ cups water
½ cup chopped parsley
1 bay leaf, crumbled
2 tablespoons salt
2 teaspoons thyme
Freshly ground pepper

Fry bacon until crisp. Remove and reserve bacon and all but 2 tablespoons fat. Add ground beef, breaking it up with a spoon, and cook until brown, stirring constantly. Stir in onion, green pepper and garlic and cook for 10 minutes. Add more bacon fat if needed. Mash tomatoes with a spoon. Stir tomatoes and tomato paste, bacon, 1 cup wine, 4 teaspoons each oregano and basil and all remaining ingredients into sauce. Bring to a boil; reduce heat and simmer, uncovered, for 3 hours, stirring occasionally. Taste after an hour of cooking and correct the seasonings; herbs vary and so do personal notions of flavor. If you make the sauce early, cool and refrigerate it until an hour or two before dinner. Let it warm to room temperature before you reheat it. Ten or 15 minutes before serving, blend in 1 teaspoon each of oregano and basil and ½ cup wine. Serve over spaghetti. *This recipe may be doubled and freezes well.*

Alma Elton
St. Clair County (Osceola)

ITALIAN SPAGHETTI SAUCE AND MEATBALLS

1 pound ground beef
½ pound ground pork
2 tablespoons vegetable oil
1 medium onion, chopped
2 cloves garlic, minced
½ green pepper, minced
1 large or 2 small cans tomatoes
2 small cans tomato sauce
2 sauce cans water
2 tablespoons parsley flakes
2 basil leaves, fresh or dried (½ teaspoon if ground)
½ teaspoon thyme
Salt and pepper to taste
¼ teaspoon crushed red pepper

Brown meat in oil and add onion, garlic and green pepper. After cooking to steaming point, add tomatoes, sauce and water and dry ingredients. Cook 1½ to 2 hours or until as thick as desired. If you want to make meatballs to use in sauce, omit meat. Make meatballs by using same amount of meat, half the amounts of garlic, onion and parsley and add 2 tablespoons grated Italian cheese. Make 1-inch balls, brown lightly, stir gently into the above sauce and cook about ½ hour to 45 minutes. *I got this recipe years ago from an Italian brother-in-law and, as a service wife, it traveled all over the world with me as a company special dish.*

Mrs. James R. Taylor (Jerri)
Oregon County (Alton)

RAVIOLI

Meat filling:

2 tablespoons onion
2 tablespoons butter
2 pounds beef chuck roast, cut up
1 pound pork butt roast, cut up
1 cup celery
¼ cup parsley
2 cloves garlic
¼ cup onion
1 teaspoon sage
Salt and pepper to taste
1 (20-ounce) can spinach
3 eggs
½ cup breadcrumbs

Brown onions in butter. Add cut up meat and brown. Add water to cover meat. Add celery, parsley, garlic, onions, sage, salt and pepper. Cook about 3 hours or until very done. Drain and save juice for sauce. Grind cooked meat with spinach; add eggs, breadcrumbs, salt and pepper until moist enough to spread.

Pasta:

4 eggs
1 tablespoon salt
½ cup vegetable oil
5 cups lukewarm water
5 pounds or more flour

Mix all ingredients together until sticky but holds together. Reserve ½ the pasta and repeat the next steps with it. Knead in flour until elastic, then roll on floured board to thin and even shape. Reserve ½ the meat filling to be used with the reserved pasta. Now spread the remaining meat filling about ⅛ inch thick over ½ the pasta on the board. Lift and pull the other side of the pasta over the side spread with the meat filling. Seal edges with pie crust cutter, then trace with rolling pin tracer (or use yardstick crisscross to make 1-inch squares) pressing firmly to seal. Cut with pie crust cutter, then place on floured paper towels to dry 24 hours, turning once. May be frozen or cooked in boiling, salted water at least 20 minutes. Drain and serve with sauce and Parmesan cheese.

Ravioli (continued)

Sauce:

2 cloves garlic
1½ tablespoons parsley
1½ tablespoons onion, dried or powdered
1½ tablespoons sage
1½ tablespoons celery seed
5 tablespoons butter
2 tablespoons onions
6 (10-ounce) cans tomato soup
5 soup cans juice from meat or water

Make spice bag with garlic, parsley, dried onion, sage and celery seed. Brown butter and 2 tablespoons onions. Add soup, juice or water. Put spice bag in tomato sauce and cook slowly about 4 to 5 hours. *Yield: 175 to 200 ravioli.*

Mrs. John Stefanoni
St. Louis County—Northwest Unit (St. Louis)

ORIGINAL MAIN DISH

1 pound bacon
6 to 8 potatoes
1 head lettuce
1 small onion
½ to ¾ cup light vinegar

Cut bacon with scissors in bite-sized pieces and fry until crisp. Boil potatoes until tender. Chop up lettuce and onion in large bowl. Add drained bacon pieces and cut up potatoes to the lettuce and onion. Using about ¼ of the bacon drippings, add vinegar and bring to a boil. Pour over entire mixture, mix well and serve immediately. *This is an original family favorite and is a complete meal when served with Ritz crackers and gelatin salad.*

Mary Holcomb
Grundy County (Trenton)

BIGOS (EASY HUNTER'S STEW)

¼ cup all-purpose flour
1 tablespoon paprika or caraway seed
1 pound lean beef, cubed
1 pound lean pork, cubed
2 tablespoons butter or margarine
2 pounds sauerkraut, rinsed and drained
2 medium onions, sliced
12 ounces kielbasa (Polish sausage) *or* 6 smokie link sausages, cut into 1-inch pieces
1 (4-ounce) can sliced mushrooms, undrained
½ cup dry white wine
Chopped parsley (optional)
Small boiled potatoes (optional)

Combine flour and paprika and coat pork and beef. Heat butter in a Dutch oven or saucepan. Add pork and beef and brown on all sides. Add sauerkraut, onion, sausages, mushrooms, and wine and mix well. Cover and cook over low heat 1½ to 2 hours or until meat is tender. Remove meat and vegetables to serving platter. *If desired, garnish with parsley and serve with small boiled potatoes. Makes 6 to 8 servings.*

Mrs. Charles Novak (Berniece)
Buchanan County (St. Joseph)

GOLD NUGGET MEAT LOAF

2 eggs
⅔ cup milk
2 teaspoons salt
¼ teaspoon pepper
3 slices bread, crumbled
1 onion, chopped
½ cup shredded raw carrots
1 cup shredded Cheddar cheese
1½ pounds lean ground beef
¼ cup catsup
¼ cup brown sugar
1 tablespoon prepared mustard

Gold Nugget Meat Loaf (continued)

Break eggs into a large mixing bowl. Beat slightly with fork and add milk, salt, pepper and crumbled bread. Beat until bread is absorbed with milk, add chopped onion, carrots, cheese and beef. Blend well. Pack into a loaf pan, combine catsup, brown sugar and mustard and spread over top of loaf. Bake for 1 hour at 350 degrees, uncovered. *This is my son's favorite main dish. Try it once!*

Marvis Trump
Clark County (Luray)

SWEDISH MEATBALLS

Meatballs:

1 egg, beaten
2 tablespoons minced onion
1 teaspoon salt
⅔ cup fine breadcrumbs
1 pound ground beef
1 (10¾-ounce) can cream of celery soup
Dash of parsley flakes if desired

Combine all ingredients, except ½ cup soup. Shape into small balls. Brown in skillet and place in a 9-inch container.

Sauce:

2 cups hot water
¼ cup flour
1 teaspoon paprika
¾ cup sour cream
½ cup celery soup saved from above

Mix water, flour and paprika in skillet that meatballs were browned in. Cook until thickened. Add sour cream and celery soup and pour over meatballs. Bake at 250 degrees for 20 minutes. *Yield: 6 to 8 servings.*

Mrs. Josephine Bush
Gentry County (Albany)

SAUSAGE OR HAMBURGER AND BEAN DISH

2 strips bacon, cubed, fried and drained
1 onion, finely chopped
1 pound ground sausage or ground beef
2 pounds pork and beans
½ cup molasses
½ cup catsup
½ teaspoon dry mustard
1 tablespoon Worcestershire sauce
Salt and pepper to taste

Fry the bacon; drain. Add onion to bacon. Brown sausage or ground beef and add to bacon and onion. Combine with remaining ingredients. May be cooked on top of the stove or in the oven at 375 degrees for about 30 minutes. *I've never had anyone who didn't love this quick delicious dish. Warms up beautifully, too.*

Mrs. Earl Moentmann (Virginia)
Carroll County (Norborne)

MEXICAN CASSEROLE

2 pounds hamburger
1 onion, chopped
1 (10¾-ounce) can of mushroom soup
1 (16-ounce) can whole tomatoes
1 can hot green chili peppers, chopped
2 cans Mexican chili beans
1 pound Velvetta cheese, cut up
12 frozen tortilla shells

Brown hamburger and onion. Grease a 13-x-9-x-2-inch pan. Place 6 frozen tortillas in bottom of pan. Top with half of hamburger, one can beans and half the cheese. Place remaining 6 tortillas on top, then add remaining hamburger, cheese and beans. Mix soup, tomatoes and chili peppers together and pour over top. Bake for 1 hour at 350 degrees. *Serve with tossed green salad. Yield: 8 to 10 servings.*

Sandy Wagoner
Henry County (Clinton)

CHEESE STUFFED MEAT LOAF

1 (8-ounce) package sliced process American cheese
2 eggs, slightly beaten
2 pounds ground beef
1 cup milk
1 cup rolled oats, uncooked
¾ cup chopped onion
2 tablespoons finely chopped green pepper, optional
2 teaspoons salt
¼ teaspoon pepper
1 tablespoon prepared mustard
1 teaspoon prepared horseradish

Cut cheese slices in half diagonally; save ½ cheese triangles for top of meat loaf. Finely chop remaining cheese slices. Combine chopped cheese with remaining ingredients; mix thoroughly. Press meat into buttered loaf pan (9-x-5-x-3-inches). Invert pan onto a foil covered shallow baking pan; fold foil edges up around meat loaf to hold juices during baking. Bake at 375 degrees until meat is done, about 1 hour. Two or 3 minutes before end of baking time, place remaining cheese slices on top of meat loaf to melt slightly. *If you like cheese, you'll like this.*

Mrs. Belle Schneider
St. Louis County — South County Unit (St. Louis)

ONE DISH MEAL

1 pound ground beef
1 large sliced onion
1 (16-ounce) can kidney beans, drained
1 can tomato soup, diluted with 1 cup water
2 cups raw, sliced potatoes
Salt and pepper to taste

Place ingredients in 13-x-10-inch baking dish in order given. Cover and bake at 350 degrees for 45 minutes; uncover, brown 10 to 15 minutes. *Yield: 6 to 8 servings.*

Ruth R. Maynard
Jefferson County — Jefferson South Unit (DeSoto)

MOM'S CABBAGE ROLLS

2 heads cabbage
3 pounds ground chuck
1½ cups instant rice
2 teaspoons salt
¾ teaspoon pepper
3 eggs
¾ cup finely chopped onion
¾ cup finely chopped water chestnuts or almonds
Tomato juice (or diluted tomato sauce)
Salt to taste
Fresh lemon juice

Clean, core and steam whole cabbage until slightly transparent. Cool and separate leaves. Mix all remaining ingredients, except tomato juice, salt and lemon juice. Place small amount of meat mixture on each cabbage leaf. Wrap, placing folds on bottom. Layer in a 9-x-13-inch pan, repeating layers no more than twice. Cover with tomato juice, salt and lemon juice to taste. Bake at 275 degrees for 1½ to 2 hours or until most of juice is gone. *Note: Serve as appetizer with crackers or as a main dish.*

Mrs. Dan Sullivan (Bonnie)
Greene County (Springfield)

CHILIGHETTI

1 pound ground beef
1 large chopped onion
2 teaspoons chili powder
2 cups kidney beans or chili beans
2 cups tomato juice
1½ cups raw spaghetti
1 tablespoon Worcestershire sauce
½ teaspoon pepper

Brown ground beef and onion with chili powder. Add other ingredients and mix well. Put in buttered baking dish. Bake at 350 degrees for 1 hour.

Mrs. Bruce Elliot (Evangeline)
Carter County (Van Buren)

HAMBURGER BAKE

- 1 pound ground beef
- 1 tablespoon shortening
- 1 large onion, minced
- 2 large carrots, grated
- 3 large stalks celery, cut into pieces
- 1 green pepper, cut into small pieces
- ½ cup raw rice
- 2 cups tomatoes or tomato juice
- Buttered breadcrumbs or cracker crumbs

Brown meat in shortening in a large skillet. Add vegetables to meat and simmer 5 minutes. Put the rice in bottom of a shallow 10-inch baking dish. Cover with meat and vegetables and pour tomatoes over top. Cover with enough water to barely cover. Bake 40 minutes at 375 degrees or until liquid is almost absorbed. Cover with crumbs and bake 5 minutes longer.

Madeleine Hicks
Scotland County (Memphis)

CHILAQUILES

- 12 corn tortillas
- 1 (10-ounce) can hot enchilada sauce
- 1 small can tomato sauce
- 1 cup shredded sharp Cheddar cheese
- ½ cup chopped onions
- 1½ cups cooked ground beef

Fry tortillas in small amount hot vegetable oil. Cut each tortilla into 4 pieces. Set aside in a large bowl. In saucepan, combine enchilada and tomato sauces; cook on low heat for 15 minutes; pour over tortillas. Combine cheese, meat and onions. Mix all of the ingredients together and bake at 350 degrees for 20 minutes. Serve hot.

Mrs. Ray Williams (Elida)
Dallas County (Urbana)

HAMBURGER ON BUNS

1 pound lean ground beef
3 tablespoons mayonnaise
2 teaspoons Worcestershire sauce
1 egg
2 tablespoons chili sauce
1 teaspoon dry mustard
1 onion, grated
½ clove garlic, minced
Salt and pepper to taste

Mix above ingredients well. Cut 8 small hamburger buns in half. Spread each half with mixture to the edge of the bun. Broil for 5 minutes. *These can be made ahead . . . a tasty treat for after the game!*

Mrs. Wilbur Bushnell (Loy)
St. Louis County — North County Unit (Florissant)

PIGS IN THE BLANKET

3 pounds ground beef
Salt and pepper to taste
¼ pound sausage
1 medium onion, diced
1 clove garlic, finely chopped
½ cup partially cooked rice
1 medium head cabbage
1 quart sauerkraut
1 quart canned tomatoes

Mix beef, seasonings, sausage, onion, garlic and rice together while parboiling cabbage. Line bottom of large roaster with layer of sauerkraut and tomatoes. Remove leaves from parboiled cabbage. Place enough meat mixture on leaves so they can be folded over. Secure with toothpick if necessary. Place folded leaves in roaster. Repeat layer of sauerkraut and tomatoes. If you need more than 1 layer of cabbage rolls, place second layer of rolls on top. Cover roaster. Bake no less than 5 hours at 350 degrees. *Yield: 6 generous servings.*

Mrs. Jarel Anderson (Velma)
Ozark County (Gainesville)

MEAT AND POTATO PIE

1½ pounds ground beef
¾ cup evaporated milk
4 slices soft bread, crumbled
1 egg
1 teaspoon salt
1½ teaspoons dry mustard
¼ teaspoon pepper
¼ teaspoon oregano
1 small onion, minced
4 ounces American cheese, sliced
1 envelope instant mashed potatoes (recipe for 4)

Mix all ingredients except cheese and potatoes together. Pack into a 9-inch pie pan. Bake at 350 degrees for 40 minutes. Remove from oven, lay cheese slices on top and pile cooked mashed potatoes on top. Bake 10 more minutes. *Yield: 8 servings.*

Zelma Pierce
DeKalb County (Maysville)

GREEN BEAN CASSEROLE

1 pound ground beef
2 cups narrow egg noodles
1 (16-ounce) can French style green beans
1 or 2 cans cream of mushroom or cream of chicken soup
¼ cup milk
1 can onion rings

Brown ground beef and set aside. Cook noodles and drain. Drain half the green bean liquid. Combine all in a 2 or 3 quart casserole dish, except onion rings. Bake at 425 degrees for 20 to 30 minutes. Sprinkle onion rings on top and return to oven for 5 minutes. *Serves 6 to 8. This is very good.*

Archie L. Jones
Osage County (Linn)

SOUR CREAM CASSEROLE

1½ pounds ground beef
Salt and pepper to taste
Garlic salt to taste
1 (8-ounce) can tomato sauce
1 (5-ounce) package wide noodles
1 pint sour cream
1 (12-ounce) carton cottage cheese
6 small green onions, chopped
2 tablespoons butter or margarine
½ cup cheese, shredded

Brown beef in butter until it loses its pink color. Add seasonings and tomato sauce. Stir to mix well. Simmer 5 minutes. Cook noodles according to package directions. Rinse and drain. Add sour cream, cottage cheese, onions and beef. Pour into large greased casserole dish or small roasting pan. Sprinkle cheese over top. Bake at 350 degrees for 25 minutes.

Mary Harris
Christian County (Ozark)

TOP OF THE STOVE MEAT LOAF

1 pound ground beef
¾ cup chopped onion, divided
2 tablespoons chopped parsley
⅔ cup milk
½ cup rolled oats
Salt and pepper to taste
2 eggs, beaten
2 tablespoons flour
3 tablespoons fat
1 can tomato soup

Mix beef, ¼ cup onion, parsley, milk, oats, salt, pepper and eggs; shape mixture into 2½-inch thick loaf. Sprinkle loaf with flour; brown slowly on both sides in fat. Sprinkle remaining onion around loaf. Cook 5 minutes. Pour soup over top; cover. Cook for 45 minutes.

Lucy Belle Martin
Marion County (Maywood)

Veal

MA'S CALIFORNIA CASSEROLE

2 pounds veal round steak
1/3 cup flour
1 teaspoon paprika
1/4 cup vegetable oil or shortening
1 medium onion, sliced and separated into rings
1 can cream of chicken soup

Cut steak into 2-inch cubes, mix flour and paprika together and sprinkle generously over meat, then pound the flour into the meat. Brown meat well in oil. Transfer to 14-x-10-x-2-inch pan and add onion slices on top. Combine soup and 1 soup can of water in skillet used for browning; bring to a boil and pour over meat. Bake, uncovered, at 350 degrees for 45 minutes or until tender.

Butter Crumb Dumplings:
2 cups sifted flour
4 teaspoons baking powder
1/2 teaspoon salt
1 teaspoon celery seed
1 teaspoon dry onion flakes
1/4 cup vegetable oil or butter
1 cup milk
1/4 cup melted butter
1 cup breadcrumbs

Sift flour, baking powder and salt; add celery seed, onion flakes, oil, and milk. Stir until moistened. Drop rounded teaspoon of dough into mixture of melted butter and breadcrumbs. Roll to coat with crumbs. Place dumplings on top of cooked meat and bake, uncovered, at 425 degrees for about 20 minutes or until deep golden brown. *I like more gravy so I add an extra can of soup and an extra can of water to meat just before adding dumplings. Also make dumplings small. Serves 8.*

Mrs. Doyle Williams (Anne)
Dunklin County (Kennett)

Pork

COMPANY LASAGNE

1 pound Italian sausage
1 clove garlic, minced
1 tablespoon basil leaves
1½ teaspoons salt
2 cups cooked tomatoes
1 (12-ounce) can tomato paste
1 package lasagne noodles
3 cups creamy cottage cheese
½ cup grated Parmesan cheese
2 tablespoons parsley flakes
2 beaten eggs
1 teaspoon salt
½ teaspoon pepper
1 pound mozzarella cheese, sliced thin

Brown meat slowly; spoon off excess fat. Add next 5 ingredients to meat and simmer, uncovered, for 30 minutes. Stir occasionally, adding small amount of water as needed. Cook noodles in large amount boiling, salted water until tender; drain and rinse. Combine remaining ingredients except mozzarella cheese. Place half the noodles in a 13-x-9-inch baking pan; spread with half the cottage cheese filling; add half the mozzarella cheese and half the meat mixture. Repeat the layers. Bake at 350 degrees about 30 to 40 minutes. Let stand 10 minutes before cutting into squares. *Serves 8. This can be assembled early and refrigerated. Be sure to allow 15 minutes longer in the oven.*

Bessie Lee Hickman
Grundy County (Spickard)

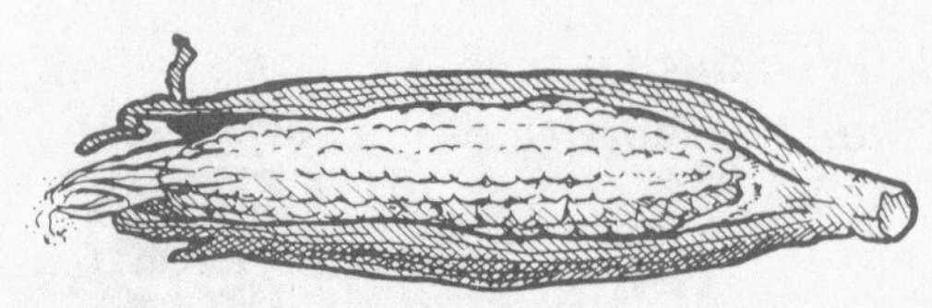

APRICOT ROAST PORK

1 (4-pound) rolled boneless pork roast
1 teaspoon salt
¼ teaspoon pepper
¼ cup brown sugar
1 cup apricot preserves
1 medium-sized can apricot halves
Few sprigs parsley (optional)

Place roast, fat side up, in roasting pan. Sprinkle with salt and pepper. Place in oven at 325 degrees for 30 to 40 minutes per pound. About 45 minutes before end of roasting time, spread the mixture of brown sugar and apricot preserves over surface of roast. You may test for doneness by cutting into center of roast; meat should have lost all pinkness and be white or grayish. When meat is well done, remove to cutting board. Add can of apricot halves and juice to drippings in pan; place back in oven to warm thoroughly. Slice roast in thin slices and arrange on platter. Garnish with apricot halves around the edge. Drizzle some of the liquid drippings over the sliced meat for added flavor. Sprigs of parsley add a touch of color. *Yield: 6 to 8 servings. Note: Size of roast can be increased according to number of guests.*

Shirley Boehm
Gasconade County — Gasconade South Unit (Hermann)

Stick a toothpick in the whole clove of garlic when making chili, etc. The toothpick makes it easier to find and remove before serving.

BARBECUED RIBS

2 tablespoons vegetable oil
1 cup chopped onion
1 cup tomato catsup
¼ cup wine vinegar
2 tablespoons Worcestershire sauce
1½ teaspoons sugar
1 teaspoon salt
1 teaspoon black pepper
2 teaspoons chili powder
¼ teaspoon paprika
1 cup water
4 pounds ribs, cut into pieces

Combine all ingredients for sauce and cook on low heat until onions are tender, approximately 15 minutes. Brown ribs in oven at 450 degrees on both sides; drain. Pour sauce over ribs and bake at 350 degrees for 1 hour.

Mrs. R. H. Summers (Virginia)
Howard County (Fayette)

SPANISH PORK CHOPS

6 pork chops, 1 to 1½-inches thick
1 tablespoon salt
1 chopped green pepper
1 (4-ounce) jar stuffed olives, sliced with juice
1 (20-ounce) can tomatoes
½ teaspoon Worcestershire sauce
Salt and pepper to taste
¾ cup raw rice
¾ cup water

Place salt in bottom of pan and brown pork chops in same pan. Mix together the green pepper, olives, tomatoes, Worcestershire, salt and pepper, rice and water and pour over chops, which have been placed in a large baking dish (12-x-12-inch). Cover tightly with foil and bake at 325 degrees for 1 hour.

Cecelia A. Walsh
Wright County (Mountain Grove)

SWEET AND SOUR PORK

1½ pounds pork, cubed
2 cups water
¼ cup soy sauce
2 tablespoons sugar
2 medium tomatoes, cut into pieces
1 green pepper, diced
½ cup green onions, chopped
⅔ cup pineapple chunks, reserve juice
¼ cup butter

Simmer pork in water, soy sauce and sugar for 1 hour; drain. Remove seeds and juice from tomatoes and combine with green pepper, green onions, and pineapple. Cook in butter to keep vegetables crisp. Dip pork in batter and fry until brown. Arrange pork on platter. Mix with vegetables. Pour sweet and sour sauce over all.

Batter:
1 egg, beaten
⅔ cup milk
1 cup sifted flour
2 teaspoons baking powder
½ teaspoon salt
¼ teaspoon MSG

Combine egg and milk. Add sifted dry ingredients. Beat until smooth.

Sweet and sour sauce:
½ cup vinegar
½ cup water
¼ cup brown sugar
¼ cup granulated sugar
¼ cup cornstarch
½ cup pineapple juice

Combine vinegar, water, brown sugar and granulated sugar to a boil. Combine cornstarch and pineapple juice. Add hot mixture and cook until thickened.

Ruth Doublin
Stoddard County (Puxico)

IRRESISTIBLE PORK CHOPS

1 (8-ounce) can crushed pineapple, drained
1 cup brown sugar
Juice of 1 lemon
1 tablespoon prepared mustard
1 teaspoon dry mustard
Dash of salt
6 pork loin chops, cut 1½ inches thick
Pineapple slices
Maraschino cherries

In blender container, add crushed pineapple, brown sugar, lemon juice, mustards, and salt; process until smooth. Set aside. Place chops on grill 4 to 6 inches above low heat coals or 6 inches above the heat on a gas grill with the heat setting on low. Cook slowly, turning frequently, about 1 hour. When chops are done, cover with 3 or 4 tablespoons of pineapple sauce. Garnish with pineapple slices; place maraschino cherry in the center of slice. Serve immediately for a prize-winning meal. *This was the 1977 Missouri Pork Cook-out first place winning recipe. It was also entered in the National Pork Cook-out in Seattle Washington.*

David L. Miller
Carroll County (Carrollton)

CREAMED LIVER

2 pounds beef or pork liver
2 cans (10-¾ ounces) cream of chicken soup
1 medium onion, sliced

Roll liver in corn meal; brown in skillet in bacon fat. Remove liver and brown onions. Pour off fat. Place liver in skillet, top with onions. Pour on soup mixed according to directions on can. Cover and simmer over low heat for 1 hour.

Sister Assunta Guittar
Cole County (Jefferson City)

PIZZA STYLE PORK CHOPS

1½ cups grated breadcrumbs
1 teaspoon salt
1/8 teaspoon pepper
1 teaspoon parsley
1 teaspoon basil leaves
1/8 teaspoon garlic salt
2 tablespoons oregano
6 pork chops
¼ cup vegetable oil
1 (16-ounce) can tomatoes
Pinches of sugar, salt and pepper
2 medium onions, sliced

Mix dry ingredients, saving 1 tablespoon oregano for later. Dip chops in oil and then coat with dry mixture. Bake in shallow pan at 350 degrees for 1 hour. While chops are baking, simmer tomatoes in saucepan with pinch of salt, sugar and pepper. Simmer tomatoes until soft and mash them while cooking. Slice onions and sauté them in 1 teaspoon oil, but do not brown them. When chops are brown, turn over and cook until other side is brown. Then spread tomatoes on top of chops and add the onion. Sprinkle with reserved oregano. *Chops should be well done in 1 hour. Drain excess fat from pan before adding tomatoes and onions.*

Katherine Schumer
Perry County (Perryville)

Poultry

SPICED CHICKEN LIVERS

1 pound chicken livers
½ cup soy sauce
½ cup green onion, chopped
¼ cup dry vermouth or sherry
1 tablespoon sugar
¼ teaspoon ground ginger

Place chicken livers in saucepan with water to cover. Bring to a boil. Drain well. Add remaining ingredients. Add water to cover. Simmer gently 20 minutes. Chill without draining. Drain before serving. Serve at room temperature.

JoAnn Kinder
St. Louis County — North Central County Unit (Florissant)

CHICKEN ENCHILADAS

1 onion, chopped
¼ cup margarine
2 cans cream of chicken soup
1 can tomatoes and chili peppers
1 can chopped chili peppers
1 large can ripe olives
2 jars pimentos
2 pounds chicken, cooked and cut up
Crushed Doritos
Shredded cheese

Sauté onion in margarine. Add soup, tomatoes, chili peppers, olives, pimentos and chicken. Combine layers of crushed chips and meat mixture. Top with shredded cheese. Bake at 350 degrees for 30 minutes or until cheese melts.

Mrs. Chester Clark
Clay County — Liberty Unit (Liberty)

RANCH HOUSE CHICKEN

1 package flour tortillas
¼ pound chicken, cut up and cooked
1 chopped green pepper
1 chopped onion
1 can cream of mushroom soup
1 can cream of chicken soup
1 can tomatoes and green chilies
Chili powder and garlic salt to taste
½ pound shredded Cheddar cheese

Put tortillas in boiling chicken broth, 1 at a time, then place in casserole dish, 13-x-9-inches. Sprinkle layer of chicken over tortillas, a layer of green pepper and onion, a layer of soups, tomatoes and green chilies and seasoning, and a layer of cheese. Repeat layers. Bake, uncovered, at 375 degrees for 30 minutes.

Mrs. C. W. Love
Mississippi County (Charleston)

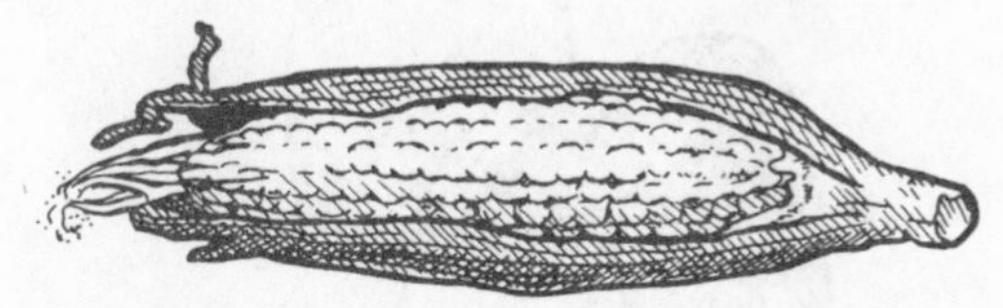

CHICKEN CURRY

1 (4-pounds or more) stewing chicken, reserve broth
2 tablespoons butter or margarine
1 cup sliced mushrooms
1 cup minced onions
1 tablespoon cornstarch
2 teaspoons salt
½ teaspoon pepper
2 tablespoons curry powder
3 cups carrots, cleaned and grated
3 sprigs parsley (optional)

Boil chicken until tender. Remove skin and bones; chop into 1-inch cubes; save broth. In deep fry pan, melt butter; sauté mushrooms until tender. Add 3 or 4 cups broth. Thicken with cornstarch. Add salt, pepper, and curry powder. Add raw carrots and cut up chicken. Cook until carrots are tender. Add parsley to top when serving. *Serves 8. Serve over fluffy rice with a tossed green salad. This is a good spring dinner.*

Mrs. John Felgate
Jefferson County — Jefferson South Unit (Festus)

CHICKEN GARDINER

1 whole chicken breast per person
Slices of boiled ham
Swiss cheese
Butter
½ cup grated Parmesan cheese
2 cups seasoned breadcrumbs
3 tablespoons sesame seeds

Bone each chicken breast and cut in half. On top of each piece, put a slice of boiled ham and a strip of Swiss cheese. Roll up and secure with toothpicks. Dip each roll in melted butter, then roll in a mixture of remaining ingredients. Place in a casserole dish and pour ¾ of basting sauce over rolls. Bake at 350 degrees for 1 hour, basting with remaining sauce every 15 minutes.

Sauce:
1 cup red currant jelly
1 (6-ounce) can frozen concentrated orange juice
¼ cup dry sherry
1 teaspoon dry mustard
⅛ teaspoon ground ginger
¼ teaspoon hot pepper sauce
1 tablespoon lemon juice

Combine all ingredients and simmer 15 minutes. Baste chicken rolls.

Mrs. Irma Laskowski
St. Louis County — South Central Unit (St. Louis)

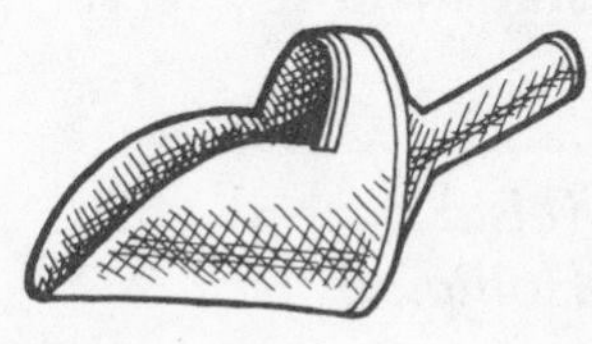

CHICKEN KIEV WITH MUSHROOM SAUCE

8 chicken breast halves
Salt to taste
1 tablespoon fresh parsley, chopped
1 tablespoon green onion, chopped
½ cup butter or margarine, chilled
1 cup all-purpose flour
2 eggs, beaten
1 cup fine dry bread crumbs

Skin and bone chicken breasts. Place each piece of chicken, boned side up, between 2 pieces of plastic wrap. Pound with a mallet, working out from the center, to form cutlets not quite ¼-inch thick. Remove plastic wrap. Sprinkle cutlets with salt, parsley and onion. Cut the butter into 8 even slices. Place a piece of butter at the end of each cutlet. Roll each cutlet like a jelly roll, butter on the inside, carefully tucking in the sides. Dust each roll with flour. Dip in beaten egg. Roll in bread crumbs. Chill 1 hour. Fry in deep hot fat (340 degrees) for about 5 minutes, or until golden brown.

Mushroom Sauce:
3 tablespoons butter or margarine
½ pound fresh mushrooms, sliced
1 tablespoon all-purpose flour
1 teaspoon soy sauce
¾ cup half-and-half

Melt butter. Add mushrooms. Sprinkle with flour. Stir to blend flour. Cook over medium heat, stirring occasionally, for 8 to 10 minutes or until tender. Add soy sauce. Slowly stir in cream. Lower heat. Simmer, stirring constantly, until mixture bubbles and thickens. Season to taste. Serve with the Chicken Kiev. *Yield: 8 servings.*

Mrs. Todd Rowe (Lisa)
Monroe County (Holliday)

SUPER CHICKEN

- 1 hen
- 1 cup celery, chopped
- 2 tablespoons onion, finely chopped
- 1½ to 2 (10¾-ounce) cans cream of chicken soup, depending on size of hen
- 1 cup mayonnaise
- 2 tablespoons lemon juice
- 1 teaspoon Dijon mustard
- ¾ teaspoons salt
- ¼ teaspoon pepper
- 1½ to 2 cups stuffing mix
- 3 tablespoons butter, melted
- 1 cup almonds, slivered

Stew hen, as desired. Skin, remove meat from bones and cut into bite-sized pieces. Combine with celery, onion, soup, mayonnaise, lemon juice, mustard, salt and pepper. Spread in baking dish. Combine stuffing with melted butter. Toss to mix well. Sprinkle over casserole. Top with almonds. Bake at 350 degrees for 30 to 40 minutes.

Jean Rohrbach
Moniteau County (Clarksburg)

OVEN BARBECUED CHICKEN

¼ cup margarine
1 onion, finely chopped
1 clove garlic, finely chopped
1 cup catsup
¼ cup vinegar
½ cup brown sugar
½ cup water
1 teaspoon salt
½ teaspoon cayenne pepper
2 tablespoons Worcestershire sauce
2 fryer chickens, cut up
Flour
Shortening

Melt margarine; saute onion and garlic. Add remaining ingredients except chicken; bring to a boil; set aside. Coat chicken with flour and brown in hot shortening. Place browned chicken in roaster and cover with sauce. Cover roaster. Bake at 350 degrees for 30 minutes; uncover chicken; bake 30 minutes longer. *May use Louisiana Hot Sauce in place of cayenne pepper. Yield: 4 to 6 servings.*

Mrs. Maurice Harlan
Marion County (Durham)

CHICKEN CASSEROLE

1 (10¾-ounce) can cream of chicken soup
1 (10¾-ounce) can cream of mushroom soup
1 (13-ounce) can Milnot
1 (5-ounce) can Chinese noodles
1 cup celery, finely chopped
1 cup cheese, shredded
3 cups cooked chicken, cut into bite-sized pieces
Buttered cracker crumbs

Combine all ingredients. Mix thoroughly. Pour into greased 12-x-8-inch casserole. Cover with buttered cracker crumbs. Bake at 300 for 45 minutes.

Elsa E. Cokely
Clay County — Liberty Unit (Liberty)

CHICKEN HUNTINGTON

10 chicken breast halves
Salt and pepper to taste
1 bay leaf
1 cup onion, finely chopped
1 cup green pepper, finely chopped
½ cup butter or margarine, melted
5 to 6 chicken bouillon cubes
1 (12-ounce) package noodles
1 cup mushroom pieces
6 to 8 stuffed green olives, sliced
2 tablespoons lemon juice
¾ (8-ounce) jar Cheez Whiz
1 (10¾-ounce) can cream of mushroom soup

Place chicken breasts in water to barely cover with salt, pepper and bay leaf. Cook over low heat until chicken is tender. Cool in broth. Reserve broth. Slice meat off bones. Sauté onion and green pepper in butter until vegetables are tender. Add bouillon cubes to reserved broth. Add noodles to broth and cook until done. Remove noodles. Add remaining ingredients to noodles. Mix well. Layer into greased casserole dish with sliced chicken.

Exis Hall
Iron County (Ironton)

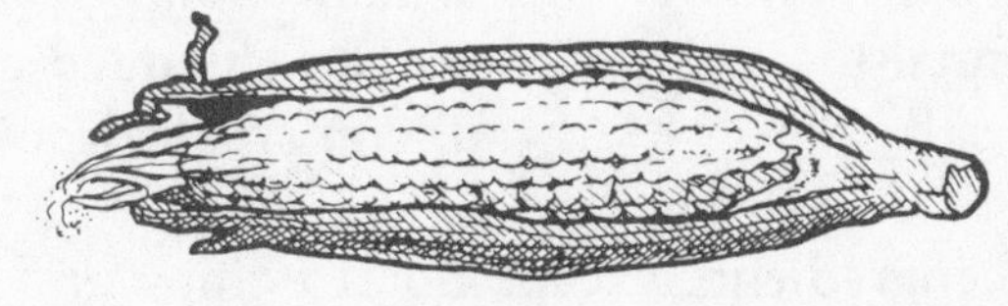

CHICKEN ORIENTAL

2½ to 3 pounds chicken
1 can cream of mushroom soup
1 can cream of chicken soup
2 tablespoons chopped onion
1 (4-ounce) can mushrooms
1 can water chestnuts
1½ cups diced celery
1 teaspoon seasoned salt
Dash of cayenne pepper
1 can English peas (optional), well-drained
1 large can Chinese noodles
1 package sliced almonds or broken cashew nuts

Cook chicken, debone, cut into chunks; discard skin. Reserve stock. Mix together soups, onion, mushrooms, water chestnuts, celery, salt and pepper. Mix with chicken. Add peas if desired. If the mixture looks too thick, add ½ cup chicken stock. Fold in half the Chinese noodles. Put in large casserole dish, sprinkle with remaining noodles and almonds. Bake at 350 degrees about 30 minutes or until bubbly. *If made the day before, do not add noodles until ready to bake.*

Mrs. Mildred Lewis
Butler County (Poplar Bluff)

CHICKEN CASSEROLE

2 cups cooked chicken
2 cups chopped celery
½ cup toasted almonds
1 cup mayonnaise
½ teaspoon salt
½ teaspoon MSG
2 tablespoons minced onion
2 tablespoons lemon juice
½ cup shredded cheese
1 cup crushed potato chips

Combine all ingredients except potato chips and cheese. Pile lightly in a 9-inch square baking dish. Sprinkle with cheese and chips.

Ruth S. Moffett
Cass County (Raymore)

CHICKEN TETRAZZINI

3 (6-pound) hens
¾ cup chopped pimento
2 tablespoons chopped parsley
2 pounds spaghetti
1½ gallons boiling water
3 tablespoons salt
2 tablespoons vegetable oil (to prevent foaming)
1½ cups margarine
1½ cups finely chopped onion
1 pound can sliced mushrooms, drained
1¼ cups flour
2 quarts milk
1 quart chicken stock or broth
¾ pound shredded cheese

Cook hens (should yield approximately 6 pounds cooked meat); dice chicken and add pimento and parsley. Cook spaghetti in salted boiling water with oil and rinse with clear water to remove all excess starch; drain. Sauté onions and mushrooms in margarine. Blend flour and salt in margarine mixture. Add milk and chicken stock. Cook and stir until smooth and thick. Combine cooked spaghetti, chicken and sauce. Place in two 12-x-20-x-2-inch or four 9-x-13-x-2-inch pans. Sprinkle shredded cheese over each pan. Bake at 350 degrees until heated through and cheese melts, about 30 minutes. *Serve with green salad and/or fruit bowl, green vegetable, rolls. Serves 50.*

Rebecca Sharp Catering Service
New Madrid County (New Madrid)

CHICKEN SPECTACULAR

3 cups cooked chicken, cut in bite-sized pieces
1 package Uncle Ben's combination wild and long grain rice, cooked in chicken broth
1 (10¾-ounce) can cream of celery soup
1 (2-ounce) jar pimentos, sliced
1 medium onion, chopped
2 cups French-style green beans
1 cup mayonnaise
1 (8-ounce) can water chestnuts, drained and chopped
Salt and pepper to taste

Mix all ingredients. Pour into greased casserole. Bake at 350 degrees for 25 to 30 minutes. Yield: 6 to 8 servings. *May be frozen before cooking.*

Christine Goodman
Madison County (Fredericktown)

CHICKEN AND RICE

1 chicken
2⅔ cup instant rice
½ cup margarine
2 (10¾-ounce) cans cream of chicken soup
2⅔ cups broth or water
¼ cup onion flakes
4 teaspoons poultry seasoning
1 teaspoon sage

Cook chicken and remove meat from bone. Place chicken and rice in large casserole dish. In a large pan, combine remaining ingredients and bring to a boil. Pour over meat and rice in dish. Mix lightly. Cover and bake at 375 degrees for 30 minutes.

LaVerne Cook
Bates County (Butler)

CASHEW CHICKEN WITH RICE

- 2 tablespoons butter
- 2 tablespoons bacon drippings
- 1 cup chopped onions
- 2 cups chopped celery
- 1 cup chopped green pepper
- ½ cup chopped red pepper
- 1 teaspoon salt
- 5 teaspoons soy sauce
- 1 can cream of mushroom soup
- 1 cup water
- 1 cup rice
- 1 medium-sized uncooked chicken, deboned
- ¾ cup canned evaporated milk
- 1 cup flour
- 2 cups bacon drippings or vegetable oil
- 1 cup cashew nuts

Melt butter and bacon drippings in skillet. Add the onions, celery, peppers and seasonings. Sauté for 10 minutes. Add mushroom soup, water and rice. Cook on low heat, covered, for 30 minutes, stirring occasionally. Add more water if needed. While the rice mixture is cooking, debone chicken and cut into 1-inch cubes. Dip in milk, then in flour. Fry in bacon drippings or oil until golden brown. Drain on layer of newspapers covered with a paper towel. Stir cashews into hot drippings for 1 minute. Drain and mix with the chicken. Arrange chicken and cashews over the rice mixture and serve while hot. *This original recipe won second place in the 1979 Lebanon Daily Record of Recipes contest.*

Mrs. Jeannette Sell Pickering
Laclede County (Lebanon)

CHICKEN BREASTS IN SOUR CREAM

4 chicken breasts
1 (4-ounce) can sliced mushrooms, drained
1 cup sour cream
1 (10¾-ounce) can cream of mushroom soup
½ soup can sherry
Paprika

Arrange chicken in shallow baking dish so that pieces do not overlap. Cover with mushrooms. (Do not use juice.) Combine mushroom soup, sherry and sour cream. Stir until well-blended. Pour over chicken, completely covering it. Dust with paprika. Bake at 350 degrees for 1 to 1½ hours.

Diane Picht
Warren County (Warrenton)

HALF AND HALF CHICKEN BREASTS

1 cup butter or margarine
12 boned chicken breasts
12 slices boiled ham
2 large onions, chopped
2 cups fresh mushrooms, sliced (may use canned)
1 teaspoon paprika
1 teaspoon salt
2 dashes nutmeg
2 pints half-and-half cream
½ cup Parmesan cheese

Melt butter in skillet. Lightly fry chicken breasts. Wrap each breast in a slice of ham and place in a large baking pan. Sauté onions and mushrooms; add seasonings. Pour onion mixture over ham-wrapped chicken. Add half-and-half to cover chicken. Simmer on top of stove for 10 minutes; bake at 325 to 350 degrees for 1 hour, longer if breasts are large. Watch closely. Sprinkle with cheese just before serving. Serve liquid left in baking pan as gravy over rice or noodles.

Maxine Bequette
St. Francois County (Farmington)

BAKED CHICKEN SALAD

3 cups diced cooked chicken
1 cup sliced celery
1 cup shredded Cheddar cheese, divided
¼ cup chopped ripe olives
1 tablespoon chopped onion
1 teaspoon salt
Salad dressing
1 cup crushed potato chips

Combine chicken, celery, ½ cup cheese, olives, onion and salt. Use enough salad dressing to moisten and toss lightly. Pour into a 1½-quart casserole dish. Sprinkle remaining ½ cup cheese and the potato chips over the top. Garnish with tomato wedges. Bake at 350 degrees for 25 minutes. *Chopped or sliced pimento may be added, if desired.*

Mrs. Donal Hall
Barry County (Cassville)

CHICKEN PARMESAN

¼ cup fine dry breadcrumbs
¼ cup grated Parmesan cheese, divided
¼ teaspoon oregano
Dash garlic powder
Dash pepper
2 pounds chicken parts
1 (10¾-ounce) can cream of mushroom soup
½ cup milk
Paprika

Combine crumbs, 2 tablespoons Parmesan cheese, oregano, garlic powder and pepper. Roll chicken in mixture. Arrange in 2-quart shallow baking dish. Bake at 400 degrees for 20 minutes; turn; bake 20 minutes more. Meanwhile, blend soup and milk. Pour over chicken. Sprinkle with paprika and remaining Parmesan cheese. Bake 20 minutes more or until chicken is tender. *When making a double recipe, I have substituted 1 can Cheddar cheese soup for 1 can cream of mushroom soup. Makes it doubly delicious.*

Mrs. Harry Panhorst (Jean)
Franklin County (Gerald)

CHICKEN AND BROCCOLI

4 to 6 chicken breasts, cooked, boned and cubed
1 (10-ounce) package frozen chopped broccoli, cooked
1 package Pepperidge Farm dressing mix, divided
1 cup mayonnaise
2 (10¾-ounce) cans cream of chicken soup
½ teaspoon curry powder or more to taste
1 tablespoon lemon juice
1 stick (½ cup) melted butter or margarine

Grease the casserole dish. Put layer of chicken, broccoli, ½ the dressing mix, then pour half the sauce over this. Combine mayonnaise, soup, curry powder and lemon juice to make sauce. Then put another layer of chicken, broccoli, the last half of the sauce, and the remaining dressing mix. Bake at 350 degrees for about 40 minutes, until bubbly. *Serves 8 to 10. This may be made ahead and frozen until the day you wish to use it. Place in the oven frozen; no need to defrost first. It will take a little longer to bake.*

Mrs. Oscar P. Rush
Cass County (Raymore)

CHICKEN AND RICE

½ cup margarine, melted
1½ cups instant rice
1 chicken, cut up
1 package onion soup mix
1 (10¾-ounce) can cream of mushroom soup
1½ cans water

Melt margarine in a roasting pan large enough to hold the chicken. Spread rice on top of the melted margarine. Lay the pieces of chicken side by side on the rice. Sprinkle onion soup mix on chicken pieces. Spread soup over chicken. Pour soup cans of water on top. Do not stir the layers together. Cover tightly. Bake 1½ hours at 350 degrees. *This recipe is fast and easy and makes a great Sunday dinner. Serves 6.*

Dee Gutshall
Caldwell County (Hamilton)

VIVA LA CHICKEN CASSEROLE

4 cooked chicken breasts
1 (10¾-ounce) can cream of chicken soup
1 (10¾-ounce) can cream of mushroom soup
1 cup milk
1 medium onion, grated
1 (10-ounce) can green chili salsa
5 to 6 tablespoons chicken bouillon
12 corn tortillas
1 pound shredded Cheddar cheese

Cook chicken and remove skin and bones. Cut into large pieces. Mix together the soups, milk, onion and chili salsa. Grease a 2½ quart casserole. Add chicken bouillon to make ½ inch layer in bottom of casserole. Break 4 of the tortillas into squares and cover bottom of casserole. Add ⅓ chicken in a layer; then ⅓ sauce. Repeat layers of tortillas, chicken and sauce 3 times, ending with sauce. Top with cheese. Refrigerate for 24 hours. Bake, uncovered, at 300 degrees for 1 to 1¼ hours. *Serves 8. Freezes well.*

Mrs. Dean Phillips (Betty Jo)
Lewis County (Lewistown)

Seafood

CHAMPIGNON AMANDINE

½ cup wild rice
½ cup long grain rice
1 cup chopped onion
1 cup chopped celery
1 cup chopped green pepper
1 (8-ounce) can sliced mushrooms, drained
2 pounds shelled, cooked shrimp
1 (6-ounce) can crabmeat, flaked
Salt and pepper to taste but sparingly
1 (10¾-ounce) can cream of mushroom soup
½ pound shredded sharp cheese
2 cups medium white sauce
¼ cup almond halves

Cook wild rice 1 hour according to package directions. Cook long grain rice separately according to package directions. Sauté vegetables together until onions are transparent, but not brown. Combine and mix well with rices, shrimp, crabmeat, salt and pepper and mushroom soup. Pour into a flat casserole (9-x-13-inch or larger). Cover with cheese. Pour white sauce over cheese. Do not stir! Brown almonds in butter and sprinkle over top. Bake at 350 degrees for 40 minutes or until heated through. Serves 10. *I like to serve this with a layered lettuce salad and white wine. A New Orleans chef parted with this recipe for $50 in 1955.*

Nancy Jo Day
Cole County (Jefferson City)

PASTA CON PESCE

1 pound pasta of your choice
1 pound unsalted butter
1 peeled and seeded fresh tomato
1 cup sliced fresh mushrooms
5 ounces lobster meat
5 ounces shrimp
5 ounces crabmeat
2 tablespoons chopped fresh parsley

Cook pasta until almost done; drain. Add butter, tomatoes, mushrooms. Stir well; add seafood. Season to taste. Sprinkle parsley on top. Serve on preheated platters. *Yield: 4 servings.*

Tony's Restaurant
St. Louis County — Central Unit (St. Louis)

ECUADORIAN SHRIMP CEBICHE (SEE-BE-CHE) OR APPETIZER

1 pound fresh or frozen shrimp, raw and deveined
Juice of 2 navel oranges
Juice of 2 lemons
2 onions, sliced ¼-inch thick
1 cup catsup
2 medium tomatoes, chopped
Fresh parsley, chopped

Put shrimp in lemon juice, orange juice, catsup, onions, and tomatoes in a container and marinate for 4 hours or overnight. Serve as an appetizer or snack with popcorn, using a sprinkling of parsley for color. *If this does not seem zesty enough, add 1/8 teaspoon garlic salt, and 2 or 3 dashes of hot sauce. Rod is an A.F.S. Exchange student from Quito, Ecuador, now living in Unionville.*

Rodrigo Guzman
Putnam County (Unionville)

PERFECT SCALLOPED OYSTERS

1 pint oysters
2 cups cracker crumbs, medium to coarse
½ cup melted butter or margarine
½ teaspoon salt
Dash of pepper
¾ cup cream
¼ cup oyster liquor
¼ teaspoon Worcestershire sauce

Drain oysters, saving liquor. Combine crumbs, butter, salt and pepper. Spread ⅓ of the buttered crumbs in a greased 8-inch round pan. Cover with half the oysters. Using another third of the crumbs, spread a second layer; cover with remaining oysters. Combine cream, oyster liquor and Worcestershire sauce. Pour over oysters. Top with last of crumbs. Bake at 350 degrees for 40 minutes. *Makes 4 to 6 servings.*

Mrs. Kay Kordes
Daviess County (Gallatin)

SUMMER SALMON

1½ cups mayonnaise
¼ cup milk
1 tablespoon onion, chopped
½ teaspoon dill weed
2 cups lettuce, shredded
2 cups shell macaroni, cooked and drained
½ cup pitted ripe olives, halved
2 cups tomato, chopped
2 cups cucumber, sliced and halved
1 (15-ounce) can salmon, drained and flaked

Combine mayonnaise with milk, onion and dill weed. Mix well and chill. In 3-quart bowl, layer lettuce, macaroni combined with olives, tomato, cucumber and salmon. Top with ¾ cup dressing. Garnish with dill, if desired. Serve with remaining dressing. *Yield: 6 to 8 servings.*

Miss Betty Radcliffe
Stone County-North (Crane)

SHRIMP AND OKRA GUMBO

1 pound fresh okra (or frozen)
2 tablespoons olive oil
¼ cup butter or margarine
2 cups diced onion
2 green peppers, seeded and diced
2 cloves garlic, minced
¼ cup all-purpose flour
1 (16-ounce) can whole tomatoes, cut up
2 cans chicken broth
2 cups water
2 bay leaves
½ teaspoon thyme
1 tablespoon hot sauce
1 tablespoon Worcestershire sauce
2 teaspoons salt
1 pound fresh shrimp, shelled and deveined or 1 (10-ounce) package frozen, shelled and deveined shrimp
Hot cooked rice

Wash and dry okra, cut into 1/8 inch slices. Heat olive oil and margarine in heavy saucepan over medium heat. Sauté okra, onion, green peppers and garlic for several minutes, stirring frequently. Sprinkle with flour. Stir until flour becomes brown. Add tomatoes, chicken broth, water, bay leaves, thyme, hot sauce, Worcestershire sauce and salt. Bring to a boil and simmer 45 minutes. Add shrimp and cook 5 minutes longer. Put a heaping spoonful of rice in each soup bowl and ladle gumbo over rice. *Serve with French bread. Yield: 8 servings.*

Mrs. Robert Eddy (Louise)
Jasper County (Carthage)

Use a tea ball for the spices for clear soups or boiled shrimp or crab legs.

LOBSTER ALBANELLO

2 pounds fresh lobster meat
1 pound fresh mushrooms, sliced
Butter
6 shallots
4 ounces fish stock
1 quart heavy cream
About 8 ounces dry white wine

Sauté lobster meat and mushrooms in butter with shallots. Add fish stock, heavy cream and wine. Cook until sauce is blended well.

Tony's Restaurant
St. Louis County—Central Unit (St. Louis)

PICKLED FISH

1 quart white vinegar
5/8 cup pickling salt
2 quarts fish fillets

Pour vinegar salt over fish in large bowl. Let stand for 5 days. Stir well each day; rinse fish.

2 cups white vinegar
1¼ cups sugar
1 tablespoon pickling spices
6 to 8 peppercorns

Slowly boil ingredients together for 10 minutes. Let cool. Pour mixture over rinsed fish. Let stand for 30 minutes. Stir 2 or 3 times. Pack loosely the following: place a layer of sliced onions in bottom of pint jar, cover with fish 1 inch deep, pour enough mixture to cover fish. Alternate layers of fish, lemon slices, mixture, and onions until jar is filled. Let stand 3 or more days before eating. *Makes 4 pints.*

J. E. Johnston
Camden County (Osage Beach)

HOT CROSSED TUNA CASSEROLE

2 (6½ or 7 ounce) cans tuna, drained
1 (10-ounce) package frozen peas, thawed
1 cup sharp natural Cheddar cheese, shredded
1 cup celery slices
½ cup breadcrumbs
¼ cup chopped onion
¼ teaspoon salt
⅛ teaspoon pepper
1 cup salad dressing
1 (8-ounce) can refrigerated crescent dinner rolls

Combine all ingredients except dinner rolls. Mix well. Spoon into 10-x-6-inch baking dish. Separate dough into 2 rectangles; press perforations to seal. Cut dough into 4 long and 8 short strips. Place strips over casserole in a lattice design. Brush lightly with salad dressing; sprinkle with sesame seeds, if desired. Bake at 350 degrees for 35 to 40 minutes or until crust is golden brown. Serve with cool cucumber sauce, which has been mixed well and chilled. *Makes 6 to 8 servings. A tossed green salad and a light dessert is all that is needed to complete this meal.*

Cool cucumber sauce:
½ cup salad dressing
½ cup sour cream
½ cup chopped cucumber
1 tablespoon chopped chives
1 tablespoon chopped parsley
¼ teaspoon salt
¼ teaspoon dill weed

Mrs. Bob Bertz (Virginia)
Lafayette County (Mayview)

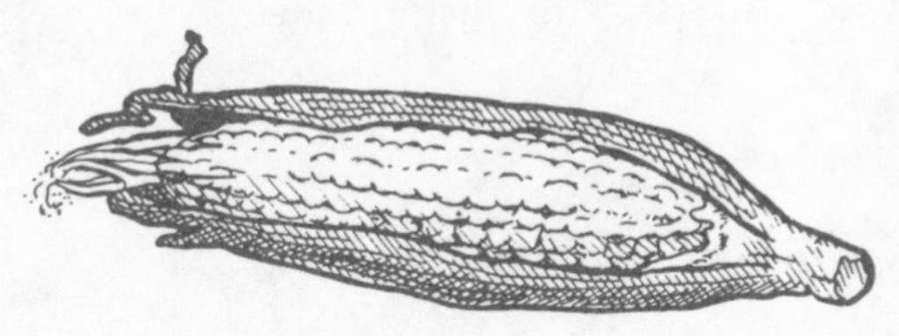

ARROW ROCK

Arrow Rock, located in Saline County 13 miles north of Interstate 70, marks the spot where the Santa Fe Trail crossed the Missouri River. It contains over 40 historic buildings, including the Home of George Caleb Bingham, one of Missouri's most famous artists.

Among the frame and red-brick buildings and the canopied boardwalk stands Arrow Rock Tavern, (pictured to the left), the oldest building in Saline County, along with a one-room jail and the old courthouse.

The Arrow Rock Lyceum, a noted summer theatre, provides excellent entertainment for visitors to this historic site.

Vegetables

THREE BEAN CASSEROLE

1 pound ground beef, cooked and drained
1 pound diced bacon, cooked and drained
1 can pork and beans
1 can green or lima beans
1 can kidney beans
½ cup barbecue sauce
½ cup brown sugar

Combine all ingredients. Bake at 350 degrees for 30 minutes in a large pan or on low heat in a slow cooker for 8 or more hours.

Rosalie Lundy
Mercer County (Princeton)

BROCCOLI-CORN BAKE

1 (16-ounce) can cream style corn
1 (10-ounce) package frozen chopped broccoli, cooked and drained
1 egg, beaten
½ cup coarsely crumbed saltine crackers
1 tablespoon instant minced onion
2 tablespoons butter or margarine, melted
½ teaspoon salt
Dash of pepper
¼ cup cracker crumbs mixed with 1 tablespoon melted butter

Combine all ingredients except buttered cracker crumbs. Turn into 1-quart casserole. Top with reserved crumbs. Bake, uncovered, at 350 degrees for 35 to 40 minutes. *Yield: 6 servings.*

Mrs. Cuna Baker
Jackson County—South Surburban Unit (Kansas City)

BROCCOLI SOUFFLE

2 eggs, well beaten
1 scant cup mayonnaise (not salad dressing
1 cup cream of celery or cream of mushroom soup
1 cup shredded Cheddar cheese
2 (10-ounce) packages frozen chopped broccoli

Mix eggs, mayonnaise, soup and cheese. Pour hot water over broccoli and let stand 5 minutes, then drain well. Combine ingredients and bake in buttered casserole dish at 325 degrees for 40 minutes or until firm. Do not overbake. *Yield: 8 servings.*

Mrs. Martha Rowe
St. Louis County—West County Unit (Chesterfield)

BROCCOLI CASSEROLE

2 (10-ounce) packages frozen broccoli, whole or chopped
½ cup chopped onion, divided
¼ cup shredded sharp cheese
1 (10¾-ounce) can cream of mushroom soup
½ cup milk
6 salted crackers, crushed
2 tablespoons margarine or butter

Cook broccoli and ¼ cup onion until tender. Drain and place in casserole dish. Mix cheese and ¼ cup onion; add soup mixed with milk. Pour mixture over broccoli. Combine crackers and melted margarine. Sprinkle on top of casserole. Bake at 350 degrees for 25 to 30 minutes or until brown and bubbly. *Makes 6 to 8 servings. Here's a creamy, mouth-watering dish I think you'll like, even if you don't usually relish broccoli.*

Mrs. Chester Koch (Dorothy)
Lincoln County (Elsberry)

BROCCOLI RICE CASSEROLE

2 tablespoons vegetable oil
½ cup chopped onion
½ cup chopped celery
1 (10-ounce) package frozen chopped broccoli
1 can cream of chicken soup
¾ soup can milk
1 small jar Cheese Whiz
1½ cups instant rice
Salt and pepper

Sauté onion and celery in oil. Add broccoli. After broccoli has thawed, cover and let simmer over low heat for 10 minutes. Add soup, milk, Cheese Whiz and rice. Salt and pepper to taste. Heat to boiling. Pour into buttered casserole dish. Bake at 350 degrees for 20 to 30 minutes. *Yield: 8 generous servings.*

Mary Wildman
Wayne County (Piedmont)

BRENDA'S CABBAGE CASSEROLE

1 medium cabbage
¼ cup butter
¼ cup all-purpose flour
½ teaspoon salt
¼ teaspoon pepper
½ cup evaporated milk

Cut cabbage into small wedges and cook in water until tender; place in a 12-x-8-x-2-inch baking dish. Melt butter, stir in flour, salt and pepper. Gradually stir in milk. Cook over medium heat until thick, stirring constantly. Pour over cabbage. Bake at 350 degrees for 20 minutes. Combine topping ingredients and spoon over cabbage. Return to oven and bake for 20 minutes longer.

Topping:
½ cup chopped green pepper
¼ cup chopped onion
⅔ cup shredded Cheddar cheese
½ cup mayonnaise
3 tablespoons chili sauce

Combine all ingredients and pour over cooked cabbage as above.

Jessica Williams
St. Louis County—North City Unit (St. Louis)

BAKED CABBAGE

6 slices white bread
2 cups milk
3 eggs, slightly beaten
1 teaspoon salt
1 teaspoon pepper
2 tablespoons grated onion
4 cups shredded cabbage
½ cup shredded sharp Cheddar cheese

Soak bread in milk for 5 minutes. Add eggs, salt and pepper, grated onion, cabbage and mix well. Put in oiled baking dish and top with shredded cheese. Bake at 350 degrees for 40 minutes. *Serves 8 to 10.*

Marjorie Heinike
Adair County (Kirksville)

CARROTS PARMESAN

20 large carrots, cut into 3 or 4 pieces
1 teaspoon sugar
1½ pints (3 cups) heavy cream
1½ cups Parmesan cheese
Salt and pepper to taste
1 onion, grated
20 pecans, halved

Boil carrots until tender in salted water to which sugar is added. Drain and finely chop or put through a food mill. Stir in cream and cheese. Season to taste. Pour into large greased casserole dish. Spread grated onion on top and arrange pecan halves over all. Bake at 350 degrees for 45 minutes to 1 hour. *Yield: 8 servings. An unusual way to glorify a carrot!*

Mrs. Martha Rowe
St. Louis County — West County Unit (Chesterfield)

HOLIDAY CARROTS AND ONIONS

1 pound carrots, cut in half lengthwise
1 pound small whole onions
1 (10¾-ounce) can cream of mushroom soup
1 tablespoon chopped parsley
½ teaspoon salt
½ teaspoon pepper
¼ teaspoon paprika
½ to 1 cup toasted slivered almonds

Cut carrots in 3-inch slices. In a covered saucepan, cook carrots and onions in water to cover for 30 minutes or until tender. Drain. Stir in soup. Add parsley, salt, pepper, and paprika. Heat, stirring now and then. Garnish with almonds. *Serves 6 to 8:*

Dorothy Edler
Ste. Genevieve County (Ste. Genevieve)

CELERY CASSEROLE

- 4 cups celery, chopped on diagonal
- 1 cup cream of chicken soup
- ½ cup water chestnuts, sliced
- ¼ cup almonds, slivered
- 2 tablespoons pimentoes, chopped
- 1 cup bread crumbs, or cracker crumbs
- 2 tablespoons butter or margarine, melted

Boil celery in salted water to cover until tender. Drain celery. Combine celery with soup, water chestnuts, almonds and pimentoes. Put in lightly greased casserole. Combine bread crumbs with melted butter. Sprinkle on top of casserole. Bake at 350 degrees for 30 minutes. *Yield: 8 servings.*

Mrs. T. P. Head
Ripley County (Doniphan)

BAKED CORN EN CASSEROLE

- 1 (16-ounce) can cream style corn
- 1 (17-ounce) can whole kernel corn
- 1 large onion, chopped
- 1 medium-sized green pepper, chopped
- 1 (2-ounce) jar pimentoes, chopped
- ⅔ cup milk
- 1 egg, well-beaten
- 1 cup rolled cracker crumbs
- 1 cup Cheddar cheese, shredded
- ¼ cup margarine, melted
- 2 tablespoons sugar (or artificial sweetener)
- Salt and pepper to taste
- Red pepper to taste

Combine all ingredients. Mix well. Pour into 2-quart Pyrex casserole. Bake at 350 degrees for 1 hour. *Yield: 8 servings.*

Mrs. T. P. Head
Ripley County (Doniphan)

SUPER MACARONI AND CHEESE

1 (16-ounce) package elbow macaroni
2 eggs, beaten
Pinch of salt
¼ teaspoon pepper
2 tablespoons all-purpose flour
1½ cups milk
4 tablespoons butter or margarine
1 pound Cheddar cheese (grated)

Cook macaroni for 12 minutes. Drain and rinse with cold water. Drain well. Chill overnight. (Rinse with ice water to use same day.) Place chilled macaroni in lightly greased casserole. Combine eggs with salt, pepper and flour. Mix well and pour over macaroni. Combine milk, butter and cheese in saucepan. Cook, stirring occasionally, over low heat until butter and cheese are melted. *Do not boil.* Pour over macaroni. Mix well. Bake at 325 degrees for 30 minutes. Lower oven to 250 degrees and bake 1½ hours.

Bernice Hammonds
Jackson County — Raytown Unit (Raytown)

POTATO CASSEROLE

4 cups mashed potatoes
Salt and pepper to taste
1 (8-ounce) package Velveeta
1 cup French fried onion rings

Place mashed potatoes in lightly greased loaf pan. Salt and pepper. Place sliced cheese over potatoes. Top with onion rings. Bake at 350 degrees for 15 minutes, until cheese completely melts.

Vickie Pabst
Callaway County (Holts Summit)

APPLES AND POTATOES

2 medium potatoes
1 cup water, divided
½ teaspoon salt
3 medium apples
1 tablespoon sugar
2 strips bacon
1 small onion, chopped

Peel and slice potato, cook in ½ cup water and ½ teaspoon salt; simmer ½ hour. Peel and slice apples, add ½ cup water and simmer for ½ hour then add sugar. In a skillet render cut up bacon, add onion and cook about 5 minutes. Combine all ingredients and keep warm. Serve with breaded pork chops. *Yield: 4 to 6 servings. This is an old family recipe, used by my Grandmother Moss.*

Mrs. Wilbur Bushnell (Loy)
St. Louis County — North County Unit (Florissant)

MAKE AHEAD POTATOES

12 large potatoes
1 (8-ounce) package cream cheese, softened
1 (8-ounce) carton sour cream
1 teaspoon onion powder (optional)
¼ cup butter, melted
Dash of paprika

Peel potatoes and boil in salted water until tender. Drain thoroughly. Whip potatoes with cream cheese and sour cream, adding a little milk if necessary. Spread in 13-x-9-inch baking pan. Refrigerate or freeze, if desired. Before cooking, drizzle melted butter over the top and sprinkle with paprika. Bake at 350 degrees for 1 hour, or until thoroughly heated.

Betty Weaver
Schuyler County (Glenwood)

CHINESE FRIED RICE WITH BACON AND MUSHROOMS

3 tablespoons bacon drippings
½ cup green onions and tops
1 cup diced celery
1 cup mushrooms, sliced
3 cups cooked rice
2 tablespoons soy sauce
1 egg, slightly beaten
½ pound crisp bacon, crumbled

Heat bacon drippings in skillet; add onions and celery. Cook until tender. Add mushrooms, rice and soy sauce. Cook 10 minutes on low heat, stirring occasionally. Stir in beaten egg and cook until egg is done. Add bacon and mix well. *Extra soy sauce may be served with rice. Adds glamour and good taste to any main dish especially beef.*

LaVaunne Moore
Maries County (Brinktown)

WILD RICE CASSEROLE

1 cup wild rice
6 to 8 slices bacon
1 minced onion
2 cups chopped celery
1 (10¾-ounce) can cream of mushroom soup plus ½ can water
Salt and pepper to taste
1 chopped green pepper

Pour boiling water over rice, cool and drain. *Do this 3 times.* Brown bacon; drain and break into pieces. Brown onion and celery in bacon fat or butter. Mix rice, soup, water and seasoning. Add green pepper and pour into a 1½ quart casserole dish. Bake at 350 degrees for 1 hour. *Note: Always first wash rice thoroughly and soak in hot water for several hours. This will wash and puff up rice kernels.*

Mrs. Gerry Fuqua
Ralls County (New London)

WILD RICE CASSEROLE

1 package Uncle Ben's wild rice and long grain rice
4 slices bacon
1 medium green pepper, chopped
2 stalks celery, chopped
1 medium onion, chopped
1 tablespoon butter or margarine
1 tablespoon beef bouillon
1 (4-ounce) can mushrooms
1 (10¾-ounce) can cream of mushroom soup

Cook rice in 3 cups water. Reserve packet of spices from rice. Cook rice, covered, without stirring, until water is absorbed. Fry bacon in skillet until crisp. Drain bacon and pour off most of grease. In remaining grease, cook pepper, celery and onion until tender, over low heat. Crumble bacon into rice. Mix well and add butter and bouillon. Stir in remaining ingredients, including ½ of spice packet. Mix well. Bake in greased casserole at 350 degrees for 25 minutes covered. Uncover and cook additional 15 minutes.

Eva Norman
Schuyler County (Lancaster)

M-M-M-M-M-M SAUERKRAUT BALLS

2 tablespoons butter or margarine
½ medium onion, chopped
⅔ cup ham, chopped
¼ garlic clove, minced
1¼ cups plus 2 tablespoons all-purpose flour, divided
¼ cup chicken or beef broth
1½ cups sauerkraut, drained and chopped
½ teaspoon parsley, chopped
1¼ cups all-purpose flour
1 egg, beaten
1 cup milk
¼ loaf soft white bread, crust trimmed, chopped in pieces

Melt butter in large heavy skillet. Brown onion. Add ham and garlic. Lightly brown. Stir in 2 tablespoons flour. Cook thoroughly. Add broth, sauerkraut and parsley. Mix well. Cook a few minutes. Mixture should be stiff like a croquette mixture. Remove from skillet and cool. Form into 1-inch balls. Beat egg with remaining flour and egg. Dip each sauerkraut ball into batter, then into bread crumbs. Fry in deep fat. *Yield: 25 balls. Note: Recipe can be doubled.*

Ann Combs
Iron County (Ironton)

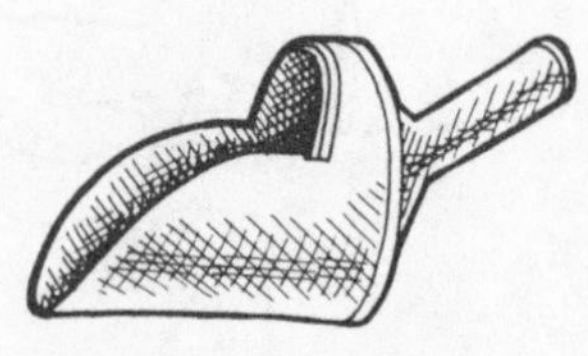

SQUASH MEDLEY

¼ cup butter or margarine
2 medium zucchini, finely chopped
1 small onion, grated
1 teaspoon basil
½ teaspoon garlic salt
2 tablespoons Parmesan cheese
1 tomato, cut into wedges

Melt butter in saucepan. Add zucchini, onion, basil and garlic salt. Stir to blend. Cover, cook over medium heat, stirring frequently, about 8 to 10 minutes, until vegetables are tender but still crisp. Remove from heat. Add tomatoes and cover. Let stand 2 to 3 minutes. Sprinkle with Parmesan. Serve immediately.

Mrs. Lois Butler
South Stone Unit (Blue Eye)

BOURBON SWEET POTATOES

4 or 5 sweet potatoes
1 cup sugar
3 eggs
½ cup butter, melted
1 small can evaporated milk
1 teaspoon vanilla
1 ounce bourbon

Cook and mash sweet potatoes. Mix with remaining ingredients. Pour into well greased casserole dish.

Topping:
1 cup pecans, chopped
1 cup brown sugar
1 cup flour
½ cup butter, at room temperature

Mix these ingredients well and sprinkle over potatoes. Bake 40 minutes at 350 degrees. *Serves 4 to 6. I made this at Christmas and some who ate it said it was good enough for dessert.*

Maxine Kirmaier
Scott County (Sikeston)

SWEET POTATO SOUFFLÉ

3 medium to large sweet potatoes
¼ cup margarine
3 eggs, beaten
1½ cups sugar
1 teaspoon cinnamon
½ teaspoon nutmeg
1 cup milk

Cook and mash sweet potatoes. Add remaining ingredients. Bake in a greased 9-x-12-inch dish at 350 degrees for 15 to 20 minutes. Remove from oven and sprinkle with topping.

Topping:
½ cup brown sugar
1 cup pecan pieces
3 cups corn flakes, crushed
¼ cup margarine

Combine sugar, pecans and corn flakes. Sprinkle over sweet potatoes. Dot with margarine. Return to oven and bake 15 minutes longer. *Yield: 10 servings.*

Helen Linhardt
Putnam County (Unionville)

BAKED ZUCCHINI

2 pounds raw zucchini
1 egg, beaten
10 to 12 double saltine crackers, crumbled
1½ cups Cheddar cheese, diced

Cook zucchini until tender. Drain and mash. Add egg. Salt and pepper to taste. Add enough saltine crackers to absorb moisture. Stir in cheese and pour into a baking dish. Bake at 325 degrees for 30 minutes.

Jean Ellsworth
Texas County (Cabool)

FETTUCINI WITH ZUCCHINI AND MUSHROOMS

½ pound mushrooms, thinly sliced
¾ cup butter, divided
1¼ pounds zucchini, scrubbed, cut julienne
¾ cup whipping cream
12 ounces fettucini
¾ cup freshly grated Parmesan cheese
½ cup chopped parsley

In a large skillet, sauté mushrooms in ¼ cup butter for 2 minutes. Add zucchini, cream and remaining butter. Bring to a boil, then lower heat and simmer mixture for 3 minutes. In a large saucepan, cook fettucini in boiling salted water for 7 minutes or until done. Drain in colander. Add pasta to skillet with Parmesan cheese and parsley. Toss with wooden fork. Transfer to a heated platter and serve with additional Parmesan cheese. *Serves 6.*

Mrs. Joel A. Montgomery (Mary Lou)
Scott County (Sikeston)

ZUCCHINI CASSEROLE

1 pound ground beef
1 medium onion, chopped
1 (16-ounce) can or 2 cups tomatoes, undrained
¾ cup water
1 envelope spaghetti sauce mix
1 teaspoon salt
1 cup precooked instant rice
3 to 4 cups zucchini squash, sliced

Brown ground beef and onions in a large skillet. Mix in tomatoes, water, spaghetti sauce mix, and salt. Bring to a boil. Stir in rice and zucchini. Cover tightly and simmer 15 to 20 minutes or until zucchini is tender. Serve hot. *Serves 6 to 8.*

Mae Burford
Washington County (Potosi)

CROCK POT VEGETABLE MEDLEY

2 cups carrots, thinly sliced and 1½ inches long
2 cups celery, thinly sliced and 1½ inches long
2 cups green beans, canned or fresh
2 cups chopped onion
2 cups cooked tomatoes
1 green pepper, thinly sliced in strips
2 tablespoons minute tapioca
1 teaspoon salt
¼ teaspoon pepper
2 tablespoons butter
½ teaspoon MSG

Prepare vegetables; add all other ingredients except MSG. Stir and place in crock pot. Cook slowly all day. Thirty minutes before serving, stir in MSG. *This can be cooking while away at work.*

Margaret Osburn
Atchison County (Fairfax)

PRETTY VEGETABLE DISH

1 package frozen baby lima beans (10-ounces)
1 package frozen peas (10-ounces)
1 (8-ounce) can French style green beans

Cook frozen vegetables according to package directions; drain. Heat drained green beans. Combine the 3 vegetables, keeping them hot.

Prepare following sauce:
1 cup mayonnaise
3 tablespoons finely chopped onion
2 tablespoons lemon juice
2 hard cooked eggs, chopped
1 teaspoon dry mustard
Few drops red pepper sauce
Salt and garlic salt to taste
Fresh bean sprouts, optional

Pretty Vegetable Dish (continued)

Mix all ingredients for sauce, retaining egg yolks to crumble over top, if desired. Pour over vegetables and toss lightly. Spoon into a 1½ quart casserole dish. Keep warm at 200 degrees. *This dish may also be served cold, if any remains! Yield: 8 to 10 servings.*

Mary R. Greim
Jackson County — Kansas City Unit (Kansas City)

VEGETABLES IN BEER BATTER

1¼ cups beer
1⅓ cups all-purpose flour
2 tablespoons grated Parmesan cheese
1 tablespoon snipped parsley
2 teaspoons salt, divided
Dash garlic powder
1 tablespoon olive oil or vegetable oil
2 eggs, separated
Vegetable oil to fill fondue pot to depth of 2 inches
1 (9-ounce) package frozen artichoke hearts, cooked and drained
1 medium zucchini, sliced
1 small head cauliflower, broken into flowerettes
1 green pepper, cut into strips

Let beer stand at room temperature until flat, about 45 minutes. Combine flour, Parmesan, parsley, 1 teaspoon salt and garlic powder. Stir in olive oil, beaten egg yolks and beer; beat until smooth. Fold in stiffly beaten egg whites. Pour oil into fondue pot to ½ capacity or to depth of 2 inches. Heat over range to 375 degrees. Add 1 teaspoon salt. Place fondue pot over burner. Spear vegetables with fondue fork; dip in batter. Fry in hot oil until golden, 2 to 5 minutes. Transfer to salad fork. *Serves 8.*

Zelma DuBois
Perry County (Perryville)

VEGETABLE CASSEROLE

- 1 (20-ounce) package frozen Parisian style vegetables-broccoli, cauliflower, carrots
- 1 (10¾-ounce) can cream of mushroom soup, undiluted
- 3 ounces cream cheese
- 1 cup shredded sharp Cheddar cheese
- 1 (4-ounce) can mushroom pieces and stems
- 1 cup crushed corn flakes
- ¼ teaspoon basil
- ¼ teaspoon celery salt
- 1/8 teaspoon thyme
- 1 tablespoon margarine, melted

Prepare vegetables according to package directions; drain. In a saucepan, heat soup, cream cheese and Cheddar cheese until sauce is smooth and cheeses melted. Combine vegetables and sauce; add mushrooms and place in a 1½ quart casserole dish. Place corn flakes and spices in plastic storage bag and crush with rolling pin. Sprinkle crushed flakes on top of casserole and drizzle with melted margarine. Bake at 400 degrees for 15 minutes or until bubbly. *Yield: 4 to 6 servings.*

Mrs. Lawrence Hoeppner
Lafayette County (Higginsville)

STIR FRIED VEGETABLES

- 3 tablespoons vegetable oil
- 2 medium carrots, cut into matchsticks
- 1 medium onion, thinly sliced
- 1 small broccoli, cut into 2x½- inch pieces
- ¾ teaspoon salt
- ½ teaspoon sugar
- ½ cup mushrooms, sliced and beef bouillon cube in ¼ cup water *or* 1 (4-ounce) can mushrooms

Heat oil in 12-inch skillet over high heat. Add carrots, onion and broccoli, stirring quickly and constantly for about 3 or 4 minutes. Add salt, sugar, and mushrooms with liquid. Lower heat. Cover and cook 5 to 6 minutes until vegetables are tender but still crisp. Stir occasionally during cooking.

Elinor Arendt
Boone County (Columbia)

VEGETABLE CASSEROLE

1 (12-ounce) can shoepeg corn, drained
½ cup onion, chopped
½ cup green pepper, chopped
½ cup celery, chopped
½ cup sour cream
1 (16-ounce) can French-cut green beans, drained
½ cup Cheddar cheese, shredded
1 (10¾-ounce) can cream of celery soup
Salt and pepper to taste
½ (10-ounce) box bite-sized Cheddar cheese crackers, crumbled
¼ cup margarine, melted
½ cup slivered almonds

Mix corn with onion, green pepper, celery, sour cream, green beans, cheese, soup, salt and pepper. Pour into buttered 8-inch square casserole, or 13-x-9-inch baking dish. Combine cheese cracker crumbs with melted margarine and almonds. Mix together well. Sprinkle over top of casserole. Bake at 350 degrees for 45 minutes. *This casserole freezes well. Freeze with topping on — just thaw and bake.*

Blanche Benham
Anrew County (Savannah)

GERMAN SCHOOL BUILDING

Built in 1871 in Hermann, Missouri, the German School Building was used as an elementary school until 1955. At that time, the building was deeded to Historic Hermann, Inc. The German School Building now houses historic and children's museums, a River Room, the Chamber of Commerce office, municipal offices, and a Tourist Information Center.

Historic Hermann, Inc. was founded in 1951. They sponsor the annual Maifest (German festival) which is held every third weekend in May.

Sweets, Etc.

Candies

CHOCOLATE FUDGE

3 tablespoons cocoa
3 cups sugar
Dash of salt
1 cup cream
½ cup light corn syrup
1 tablespoon butter
1 teaspoon vanilla extract
1 cup chopped nuts, optional

Mix cocoa and sugar and salt together. Stir in cream and syrup and mix well. Cook to soft ball stage and *do not* stir while cooking. Remove from heat and add butter and vanilla. Nuts are optional. Beat with mixer until creamy and pour into a greased flat dish. *I use my 4-quart pressure pan to cook this in. I have lots of compliments on this fudge as it does not have a lot of chocolate in it.*

Missie Good
Bates County (Amsterdam)

PEANUT BUTTER CANDY

½ cup margarine
1 cup peanut butter
1 package graham crackers, crushed
1 pound powdered sugar
2 cups chocolate chips

Melt margarine; add peanut butter. Stir in cracker crumbs, powdered sugar; mix well. (May have to use hands to mix this.) Pat onto a cookie sheet. Melt chocolate chips. Spread over first mixture. *This is very rich!*

Mrs. Oscar J. Phillips
Cooper County (Pilot Grove)

Cookies

SAND TARTS (ROLLED COOKIE)

8 cups flour, divided
4 cups brown sugar
2 cups butter
4 eggs

Roll sugar between waxed paper to remove any lumps; mix well with 7 cups flour. Work in the butter; beat eggs and mix well. Refrigerate overnight. Roll very thin, with remaining 1 cup flour if needed; cut; paint top with beaten egg and sprinkle with cinnamon and sugar, chopped nuts or an almond half. Bake at 375 to 400 degrees for 8 to 10 minutes. *Makes about 30 dozen small cookies. For Christmas cutouts, use colored sugar as trimming.*

Jeanne Wahl
Jackson County — Blue Springs Unit (Blue Springs)

SURPRISE MACAROONS

2 egg whites
1/8 teaspoon salt
1/8 teaspoon cream of tarter
1 teaspoon vanilla extract
3/4 cup sugar
1 cup chocolate chips
2/3 cup shredded coconut

Beat egg whites, salt, cream of tartar and vanilla until soft peaks form. Add sugar very slowly, beating until stiff peaks form. Fold in chocolate chips and coconut. Have ready a cookie sheet covered with brown paper. (Cut a paper sack.) Drop mixture by rounded teaspoonfuls. Bake at 275 degrees for 20 to 25 minutes, or until lightly browned. Cool slightly before removing. *Yield: 30 macaroons.*

Tracy Fairley
Sullivan County (Milan)

PINEAPPLE DROP COOKIES

½ cup shortening
½ cup granulated sugar
½ cup brown sugar
1 egg
½ cup drained crushed pineapple
2 cups flour
1 teaspoon baking powder
¼ teaspoon salt
¼ teaspoon baking soda
½ cup chopped nuts
1 teaspoon vanilla extract

Cream shortening and gradually add sugars. Add beaten egg and pineapple and blend. Sift dry ingredients together. Add gradually to first mixture. Stir in nuts and vanilla. If mixture is too stiff to drop from spoon, add a few drops pineapple juice. Drop onto oiled cookie sheet and bake at 350 degrees until light brown, about 8 to 10 minutes.

Geraldine Bird
Hickory County (Wheatland)

MOTHER'S ICEBOX COOKIES

2 cups brown sugar, firmly packed
½ cup shortening
2 eggs
3 cups all-purpose flour
1 teaspoon soda, dissolved in 1 tablespoon water
1 teaspoon vanilla
½ teaspoon salt
1 cup nuts, chopped
1 cup raisins, chopped

Cream brown sugar with shortening until light. Add eggs, 1 at a time, beating well after each addition. Add remaining ingredients, 1 at a time, mixing thoroughly after each. Form dough into long roll, wrap in waxed paper. Chill in refrigerator overnight or longer. Cut into thin (¼-inch) slices, place on greased cookie sheets, and bake at 350 degrees for 10 to 12 minutes.

Mrs. Calvin Dockery
Barton County (Lamar)

EASY FRUIT CAKE BARS

2½ cups flour
1 teaspoon baking soda
2 eggs, slightly beaten
1 (2-ounce) jar ready-to-use mincemeat
1 (14-ounce) can sweetened condensed milk
2 cups candied fruit
1 cup coarsely chopped walnuts (black or English)

Stir together flour and soda. Set aside. In a large bowl, combine remaining ingredients. Blend in flour and soda. Spread in a greased 10-x-15-inch jelly roll pan. Bake at 300 degrees for 40 to 45 minutes. Cool.

Orange glaze:
1½ cups powdered sugar
2 tablespoons orange juice

Mix until smooth. Frost cooled fruit cake bars. *Makes 48.*

Mrs. O.O. Onken (Vergil)
Scotland County (Memphis)

CHOCOLATE CRACKLES

4 ounces unsweetened chocolate
½ cup vegetable oil
2 cups sugar
4 eggs, unbeaten
2 teaspoons vanilla extract
2 cups sifted flour
2 teaspoons baking powder
½ teaspoon salt
½ cup chopped walnuts
½ cup powdered sugar

Melt chocolate in top of double boiler or in mixing bowl over hot water. Remove from heat and blend in oil and sugar. Add eggs, 1 at a time, and beat well after each addition. Add vanilla. Sift together flour, baking powder and stir into chocolate mixture. Add nuts and mix thoroughly. Chill for several hours or overnight. Shape into small balls and roll in powdered sugar. Bake on greased cookie sheet at 350 degrees for 10 to 12 minutes. *The powdered sugar coating cracks apart, giving an interesting effect. Makes about 6 dozen, 2-inch cookies.*

Betty Arnold
Ste. Genevieve County (Ste. Genevieve)

WALNUT SQUARES

1 egg
1 cup brown sugar
½ teaspoon vanilla extract
½ cup sifted flour
½ teaspoon salt
⅛ teaspoon baking soda
1 cup chopped nuts

Beat egg until foamy. Beat in sugar and vanilla. Sift flour, salt, and soda together. Add to creamed mixture and stir in chopped nuts. Spread into a greased 8-inch square pan. Bake at 325 degrees for 30 to 35 minutes or until a very dull crust. Cut into squares while still warm. Cool and remove from pan.

Mrs. Janice Jones
Dade County (Everton)

EASY PEANUT BUTTER COOKIES

1 cup peanut butter (crunchy or regular)
1 cup sugar
1 egg
1 teaspoon vanilla extract

Blend peanut butter, sugar and egg in a medium-sized bowl. Add vanilla and mix well. Form into 1-inch balls and place on an ungreased cookie sheet about 3 inches apart. Flatten with a fork, leaving a criss-cross design on each cookie. Bake at 350 degrees for 8 to 10 minutes. Remove from cookie sheet carefully, as these cookies are very tender when they are warm. *Better make a double batch of these; they disappear quickly and can be made in a hurry to serve with coffee to unexpected company. This recipe was given to me by a science teacher friend, Nancy Bane Goldman, and I remember thinking, "This will never work." But it did and the cookies taste just as good as some recipes calling for 10 or 12 ingredients.*

Nicolette Papanek
Miller County (Eldon)

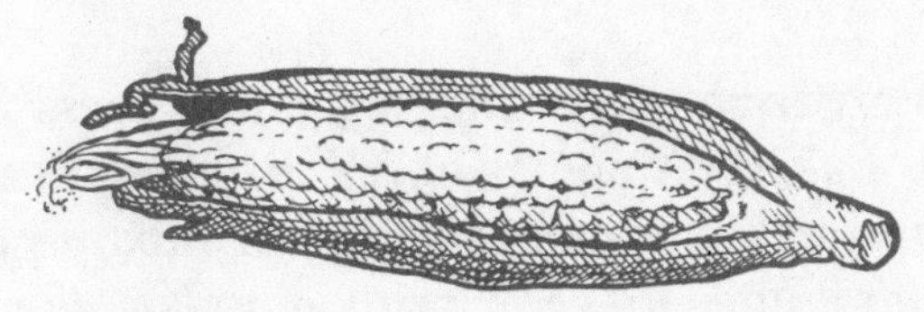

MATRIMONY CAKE (BAR)

1 cup margarine, softened
1 cup brown sugar
1½ cups all-purpose flour
1 teaspoon baking soda
1½ cups uncooked quick oats
1 teaspoon vanilla extract

Mix well the margarine, brown sugar, flour and soda. Add oats and mix well. Pat half of oatmeal mixture in greased 8-inch pan. Then add all the filling (recipe below). Finish with last half of oatmeal mixture over top. Bake about 30 minutes at 325 degrees. Cool; cut into squares or bars.

Fruit filling:
1 cup ground raisins
2 tablespoons all-purpose flour
1 cup cold water

Combine all ingredients; cook; cool. *Jelly or preserves may be used instead of raisin filling. Makes about 2 cups.*

Rosie Lucille Keith
Montgomery County (Montgomery City)

CHEWY LEMON SQUARES

1 cup margarine, softened
2 cups flour
½ cup powdered sugar
4 eggs, beaten
5 tablespoons lemon juice
½ teaspoon salt
1 teaspoon baking powder

Combine margarine, flour and sugar and press into a greased square pan. Bake 20 minutes at 350 degrees. Beat eggs, lemon juice, salt and baking powder and pour mixture over hot crust and bake 20 minutes longer. Sprinkle powdered sugar over hot squares. Cool and eat.

Shirley Yeager
Perry County (Perryville)

EAGLE BRAND COOKIES

½ cup butter
2½ cups graham cracker crumbs
1 (6-ounce) package butterscotch or chocolate chips (may use both)
1 can angel flake coconut
½ cup chopped nuts
1 can Eagle Brand sweetened condensed milk

Melt butter in 8-x-8-x-2-inch pan. Sprinkle graham cracker crumbs over butter. Layer chips, coconut and nuts in that order. Pour milk over all. Do not stir. Bake at 350 degrees for 30 minutes.

Mrs. Emmett T. Burke
Mississippi County (Charleston)

Similar recipe submitted by:
Joyce Oberle
Crawford County (Sullivan)

Keep a piece of lemon or orange zest in a jar of sugar. Use for icings or to sweeten tea.

Brownies

BUTTERMILK BROWNIES

½ cup margarine
1 cup water
¼ cup cocoa
½ cup vegetable oil
2 cups all-purpose flour
2 cups granulated sugar
½ teaspoon salt
½ cup buttermilk
2 eggs, beaten
1 teaspoon soda
1 teaspoon vanilla extract

Combine margarine, water, cocoa and vegetable oil in saucepan. Bring to a boil. Combine flour, sugar and salt in mixing bowl. Stir to blend. As soon as cocoa mixture boils, pour it over flour and sugar. Blend thoroughly. Add buttermilk, eggs, soda and vanilla. Mix well. Pour into greased and floured 16-x-11-inch jelly roll pan. Bake at 400 degrees for 20 minutes. Frost immediately with Brownie Icing. *Yield: 40 servings.*

Brownie Icing:
½ cup margarine
¼ cup cocoa
⅓ cup buttermilk
1 (16-ounce) box powdered sugar, sifted
1 cup pecans, chopped
1 teaspoon vanilla extract
Dash of salt

Combine margarine, cocoa and buttermilk. Bring to a boil. Remove from heat and add remaining ingredients. Mix well. Cover saucepan and leave on burner until ready to use.

Bernice Hammonds
Jackson County-Raytown Unit (Raytown)

DELICIOUS CHOCOLATE BROWNIES

1¼ cups sugar
½ cup margarine
4 eggs
1 (16-ounce) can chocolate syrup
1 cup all-purpose flour
½ teaspoon salt
1 teaspoon vanilla
½ cup nuts, chopped

Cream sugar and margarine. Add eggs, 1 at a time, beating well after each addition. Add remaining ingredients. Mix gently but thoroughly. Pour batter in 16-x-11-inch sheet pan. Bake at 350 degrees for 30 minutes. Cool before frosting.

Icing:
1 cup sugar
6 tablespoons milk
6 tablespoons margarine
½ cup chocolate chips
1 teaspoon vanilla

Combine all ingredients in saucepan. Heat, stirring frequently, until chocolate chips are melted. Cool.

Mrs. Flora Duncan
Andrew County (Savannah)

To sift powdered sugar evenly over cakes, use a thin strainer.

Cakes

BLACK FOREST CHERRY TORTE

Cake:

6 eggs
¾ cup sifted flour
¼ cup sifted cocoa
¼ teaspoon salt
1¼ cups sugar
1 teaspoon vanilla extract

Separate yolks from whites of eggs and allow to warm to room temperature. Sift flour once, measure, add cocoa and salt, and sift again. In small bowl of electric mixer, beat egg yolks until thick and lemon colored. Add ¾ cup of the sugar gradually and continue to beat until all has been added and the mixture is thick and light. Transfer to large mixing bowl. Beat egg whites until frothy throughout and then add ½ cup sugar gradually, beating constantly. Continue to beat until stiff peaks form. Fold into egg mixture. Sift flour mixture gradually over egg mixture, folding gently but thoroughly. Add vanilla and blend. Turn into 2 deep 9-inch layer cake pans; the bottoms of which have been lightly greased and floured. Bake at 350 degrees about 25 minutes or until cake tests done. Remove from oven and cool in pans 10 minutes.

Glaze:

1 tablespoon water
¼ cup sugar
¼ cup brandy

Combine sugar and water for glaze in a small saucepan. Place over low heat and stir until sugar is dissolved. Remove from heat and cool slightly, then add brandy. Cut cake layers from sides of pans and remove to wire racks. Brush brandy glaze over the top of warm layers and allow to cool.

Black Forest Cherry Torte (continued)

Frosting:

2 cups whipping cream
¼ cup confectioners sugar
2 tablespoons Brandy
Shaved chocolate
Merichino cherries

Combine cream and confectioners sugar and chill thoroughly. Beat until thick and light then add Brandy. Spread whipping cream on one layer of cake and top with second layer. Use remainder of cream to frost sides and top. Sprinkle with shaved chocolate and garnish with well-drained marichino cherries. Keep refrigerated.

Note: To make shaved chocolate, shave thin strips of chocolate from bar, using a swivel type vegetable peeler. Bacardi Rum may be substituted for Brandy. An 8-ounce carton of Cool Whip may be used instead of whipping cream. This dessert is great to use at organizational functions. Yield: 12-16 servings.

Mrs. Gerald Sandidge (Shirley)
Saline County (Marshall)

Decorate pies and cakes with chocolate curls made by warming a bar of chocolate in your hands, then drawing a vegetable peeler across the chocolate. Refrigerate immediately.

CHOCOLATE SOUR CREAM CAKE

1 cup sugar
1 cup sour cream
1 egg
2 cups flour
1 teaspoon baking soda
¾ cup milk
3 squares chocolate
1 teaspoon vanilla extract

Beat together the sugar, sour cream and egg until smooth. Mix flour and soda together and add to above mixture alternately with milk. Melt chocolate and add vanilla. Combine with cake mixture. Pour into a 9-x-11-inch pan. Bake at 325 degrees for 30 minutes.

Caramel Frosting:
2¾ cups sugar, divided
2 tablespoons butter
Small amount of cream

Bring 2 cups sugar and butter to a boil and boil for 1 minute. Caramelize ¾ cup sugar. Mix with the sugar/butter mixture. Beat until smooth. Frost cake in pan.

Mrs. A. B. Cooper
Mississippi County (Charleston)

Variation: For Chocolate Cake and Frosting: Mix ½ cup water and 3 tablespoons cocoa in small saucepan; cook until thick. In large bowl combine 1 cup sugar, ½ cup vegetable oil, 2 eggs, 1 cup all-purpose flour, 1 teaspoon baking powder, ½ teaspoon salt, ½ cup buttermilk, 1 teaspoon baking soda, cocoa mixture, and 1 teaspoon vanilla extract. Mix until smooth. Put in greased and floured 8-inch round pan. Bake at 350 degrees for 20 to 25 minutes. Frost with ½ pound powdered sugar, ¼ cup cocoa, ½ stick butter, softened, 1 teaspoon vanilla extract and enough evaporated milk to make spreading consistency.

Sarah Chitwood
Carter County (Van Buren)

CHOCOLATE VIENNA TORTE

6 eggs, separated
1 cup sugar, divided
¾ cup sifted flour
1 teaspoon baking powder
¾ teaspoon salt
½ teaspoon cream of tartar
¾ cup grated unsweetened chocolate
1 teaspoon vanilla extract

Beat egg yolks until thick and lemon-colored. Beat in ½ cup sugar. Sift flour, baking powder, and salt together and stir in. Beat egg whites with cream of tartar until stiff. Gradually beat in ½ cup sugar; beat until very stiff and glossy. Gently fold chocolate and vanilla into egg whites. Carefully fold egg white mixture into egg yolk mixture. Pour into two 9-inch round layer pans lined with greased paper. Bake at 350 degrees 25 to 30 minutes, or until no imprint remains when touched lightly with finger. Turn out of pans and immediately remove paper; cool. Put layers together with flavored sweetened whipped cream. Cover top and sides also. *Makes 16 servings.*

Whipped cream:
½ teaspoon gelatin
1 tablespoon cream or milk
1½ cups cold whipping cream
¼ cup powdered sugar, sifted
1 teaspoon desired flavoring

Soften gelatin in cream and dissolve over hot water. Whip the cold whipping cream until stiff. Beat in powdered sugar, the cooled gelatin and flavoring.

Mrs. Raleigh Taylor (Elizabeth)
Laclede County (Lebanon)

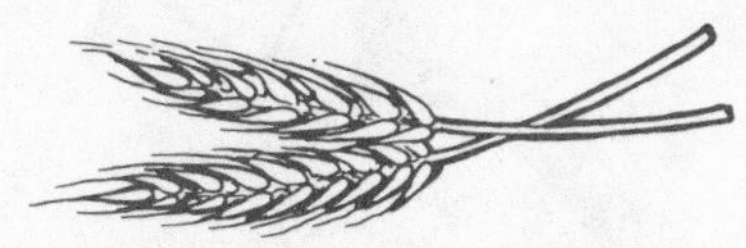

RED CAKE

½ cup shortening
1½ cups sugar
2 eggs
1 (1-ounce) bottle red food coloring
2 tablespoons cocoa
2½ cups cake or all-purpose flour
1 cup buttermilk
1½ teaspoons salt
1 teaspoon baking soda
1 tablespoon hot water
1 teaspoon vinegar

Cream shortening and sugar; add eggs, 1 at a time, and the red food coloring; then fill the bottle with water and add to mixture. Combine the cocoa and flour. Add alternately flour and buttermilk to shortening mixture. Mix together the salt, soda, hot water, and vinegar and add to batter. Bake in layer or loaf pans at 350 degrees, 25 to 30 minutes for layer, 35 minutes for loaf.

Frosting:
2 egg whites
1 cup shortening
1 package powdered sugar
½ cup butter or margarine
1 teaspoon vanilla extract

Combine ingredients in a bowl and beat with mixer until fluffy. Spread on cake. (For loaf cake, divide frosting recipe in half.)

Rosalee Merrigan
Nodaway County (Maryville)

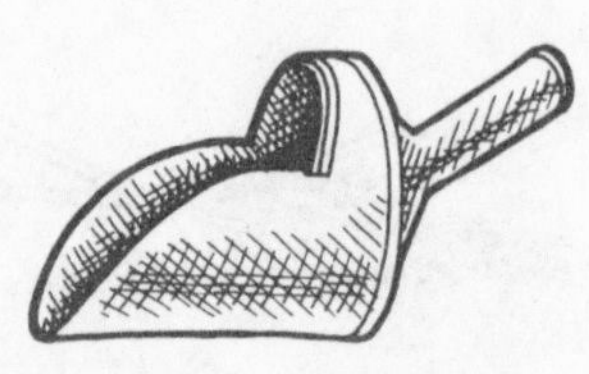

CHOCOLATE SHEET CAKE WITH NUT FROSTING

1 cup margarine
¼ cup cocoa
1 cup water
2 eggs, beaten
2 cups sugar
2 cups flour
1 teaspoon baking soda
¼ teaspoon salt
½ cup buttermilk
1 teaspoon vanilla extract

Melt margarine, cocoa, and water over low heat. Beat together eggs and sugar. Add cocoa mixture and beat. Add other ingredients and blend well. Place in 16-x-11-x-1-inch sheet pan and bake at 350 degrees for 20 minutes. Frost cake while warm.

Frosting:
½ cup margarine
3 tablespoons cocoa
6 tablespoons milk
1 pound powdered sugar
1 teaspoon vanilla extract
1 cup chopped nuts

Combine margarine, cocoa and milk in saucepan. Bring to a boil, stirring constantly. Beat in powdered sugar until smooth. Add vanilla and nuts. Spread on warm cake.

Sherrie Hogue
Gentry County (Albany)

PRALINE CHEESECAKE

Crust:

1¼ cups graham cracker crumbs
¼ cup sugar
¼ cup pecans, toasted and finely chopped
¼ cup melted butter

Combine all ingredients; press into buttered 9 or 10-inch springform pan. Bake 10 minutes at 300 degrees.

Filling:

1½ pounds cream cheese, softened
1 cup brown sugar
5⅓ ounces evaporated milk
2 tablespoons flour
1½ teaspoons vanilla extract
3 eggs

Combine cream cheese, brown sugar, evaporated milk, flour, vanilla in mixing bowl; blend well. Add eggs, 1 at a time, mixing well after each. Pour into crust. Bake 50 minutes at 325 degrees. *Paint top of cheese cake with maple syrup and/or decorate with pecans. Serves 8 to 12.*

Mrs. Roger Rowan (Susie)
Jackson County—Kansas City Unit (Kansas City)

ITALIAN CREAM CAKE

½ cup shortening
½ cup margarine
2 cups sugar
5 eggs, separated
2 cups cake flour
1 teaspoon baking soda
½ teaspoon salt
1 cup buttermilk
2 cups coconut
1 cup chopped pecans
1 teaspoon vanilla extract

Cream shortening and margarine with sugar; add egg yolks 1 at a time. Mix dry ingredients, alternately with buttermilk. Stir in coconut, nuts and vanilla; add lightly beaten egg whites. Bake in 3 layers at 350 degrees for 30 to 40 minutes.

Frosting:

½ cup softened margarine
1 package powdered sugar
1 (8-ounce) package cream cheese
1 cup chopped pecans
1 teaspoon vanilla extract

Beat until smooth and spread between layers and on top and sides of cake. *Yield: 10 to 12 servings. This cake is quite rich but delicious.*

Goldie Courtney
Chariton County (Salisbury)

Similar recipe submitted by:
Mrs. Harley McKern
Mercer County (Princeton)

WAR CAKE

2 cups sugar
2 cups hot water
¼ cup shortening
2 cups raisins
½ teaspoon allspice
2 teaspoons cinnamon
1 teaspoon ground cloves
3 cups flour
2 teaspoons baking soda
1 tablespoon hot water
Pinch of salt
1 cup nuts
1 cup applesauce

Boil first 7 ingredients for 5 minutes after it starts to bubble. Cool. Add flour. Dissolve soda in 1 tablespoon hot water; stir in pinch of salt. Combine with all remaining ingredients, mixing well. Bake in a 10-inch cake pan or two 9-x-5-x-3-inch pans at 275 degrees for 1½ hours.

Mrs. Clyde Vinyard (Louise)
Jefferson County-Jefferson South Unit (Festus)

"MA" LOCK'S WEDDING CAKE

⅔ cup shortening
1¾ cups sugar, divided
2⅔ cups cake flour
1 tablespoon baking powder
1 teaspoon salt
5 egg whites
1 teaspoon vanilla extract
1 teaspoon almond extract
1 cup milk

Cream 1¼ cups sugar and shortening together. Sift dry ingredients 3 times. Beat egg whites, adding ½ cup sugar, while beating. Mix flavoring with milk. Add alternately to flour mixture with creamed mixture. Fold in beaten egg whites and pour batter into 2 (8-inch) round or square pans. Bake at 350 degrees for 30 minutes or until done. *This recipe can be doubled but if you go more than double, you will have trouble. In doubling the recipe Ma always used larger pans and would put strips of wet terry cloth around the edges of the pans so that the outer edge of the cake would not overcook.*

"Ma" Lock's Wedding Cake (continued)

Buttercream frosting:

½ cup shortening
1 egg white
¼ teaspoon salt
1 teaspoon vanilla extract
1 box powdered sugar
Water to make spreading consistency

Mix all ingredients together in mixing bowl; beat well. Makes enough for 2 layers (8-inch). *This wedding cake recipe was originated by Mrs. Marie "Ma" Lock from a Swan's Down cake recipe and was baked the first time for her granddaughter, Rose Marie Lavelock in June, 1950. It became a tradition in the family that "Ma" would make the wedding cakes for her grandchildren and great-grandchildren as well as for the people in our community. "Ma" died when she was 82 years old. She was able to continue baking up until that time. She had made over 200 wedding cakes. When Rose Marie (Sweeney) Lavelock was learning to talk she said "Ma" for Grandma and that was the name everyone called her. "Ma's" family originated from Germany. "Ma" Lock was a wonderful, religious lady, well respected and loved and she was an inspiration to everyone that knew her.*

Mrs. Shirley Lock
Carroll County (Carrollton)

CHOP SUEY CAKE

2 cups flour
2 cups sugar
2 eggs
2 teaspoons baking soda
½ teaspoon salt
1 cup chopped nuts
1 (20-ounce) can crushed pineapple, undrained

Mix all ingredients well. Bake in a 9-x-13-inch greased and floured pan at 350 degrees for 35 to 40 minutes. While cake is hot, frost with the following frosting:

1 (8-ounce) package cream cheese
½ cup margarine
2 cups powdered sugar
1 teaspoon vanilla extract
2 tablespoons milk

Lynn Heuer
Stoddard County (Dexter)

PEPPERMINT CAKE

½ cup butter
1½ cups sugar
4 egg yolks
1 cup buttermilk
2 cups flour
2 teaspoons baking powder
½ teaspoon baking soda
⅔ cup sugar
½ cup water

Cream butter with sugar. Add egg yolks, mixing well. Add buttermilk alternately with flour, soda and baking powder; mix well. Grease and flour three 8-inch cake pans. Divide batter evenly into the 3 pans. Bake at 350 degrees until brown, about 25 minutes. Make syrup from ⅔ cup sugar and water. Spoon over layers. Make Seven Minute Frosting and as soon as you have spooned syrup over cake layers, start stacking and frosting. Sprinkle crushed peppermint candy over layers and top and sides of cake. *I use peppermint bon bon candy. Let cool. Cover in air tight container. Let stand 1 or 2 days. Very moist and pretty cake for the holidays.*

Mrs. Ruth Crain
Dunklin County (Kennett)

MISSISSIPPI MUD CAKE

2 cups sugar
½ pound butter or margarine, melted
4 eggs
1½ cups all-purpose flour
1½ teaspoons baking powder
⅓ cup cocoa
1 cup coconut
1½ cup nuts, chopped
1½ teaspoons vanilla
1 (7-ounce) jar marshmallow creme

Combine sugar with melted butter. Beat until well mixed. Add eggs, 1 at a time, beating well after each addition. Sift flour with baking powder and cocoa. Stir into butter and sugar mixture. Blend well. Stir in coconut, nuts and vanilla. Mix well. Put in greased and floured baking pan. Bake at 350 degrees for 30 minutes. Cover top of cake with marshmallow creme while cake is still hot.

Icing:
1 pound powdered sugar, sifted
⅓ cup cocoa
½ cup margarine, melted
6 tablespoons milk
1½ teaspoon vanilla
¼ cup nuts, chopped
¼ cup coconut

Combine sugar and cocoa with melted margarine. Beat until well blended. Add milk, 1 tablespoon at a time, until icing reaches desired consistency. Add vanilla. Spread on cooled cake. Garnish iced cake with nuts and coconut.

Fern Smith
Andrew Unit (Savannah)

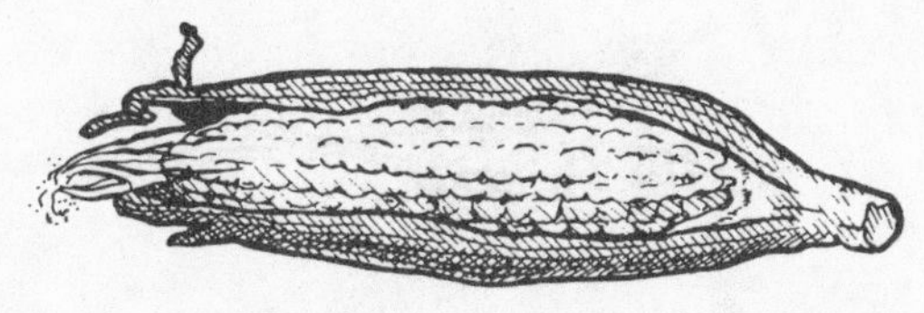

SPRING RAINBOW CAKE

1 10-inch angel food cake
1 (3-ounce) package strawberry flavored gelatin
1 (3-ounce) package lime-flavored gelatin
1 (3-ounce) package orange-flavored gelatin
2 cups strawberries, sliced in half and sweetened
½ gallon vanilla ice cream, softened
1½ cups crushed pineapple, drained
1½ cups mandarin oranges, drained

Tear cake into bite-sized pieces. Divide into 3 bowls. Sprinkle gelatin over cake, 1 flavor to each bowl. Toss cake well with gelatin to thoroughly coat cake. Place strawberry flavored cake in tube pan. Cover with strawberries. Spoon ⅓ of softened ice cream over strawberries. Layer lime flavored cake, pineapple and ⅓ ice cream. Top with orange flavored cake, oranges and remaining ice cream. Cover and freeze. Before serving, slide warm knife around outside edge to remove cake from pan. Slice and serve.

Jean Rohrbach
Moniteau County (Clarksburg)

PUMPKIN CAKE

Crust:

1 package yellow cake mix (reserve 1 cup for topping)
1 egg
½ cup butter or margarine

Mix all ingredients together and pat into 9-x-13-inch dish.

Filling:

3 cups pumpkin pie mix or 1 pound canned pumpkin
½ cup brown sugar
2 eggs
⅔ cup evaporated milk
¼ teaspoon ground cloves
½ teaspoon cinnamon
½ teaspoon salt

Mix all ingredients together and pour over crust.

Topping:

1 cup yellow cake mix
¼ cup sugar
1 teaspoon cinnamon
¼ cup butter or margarine

Mix all ingredients together and sprinkle over filling. Bake at 350 degrees for 45 to 50 minutes. *Serve with whipped cream or Cool Whip.*

Mildred Stovesand
Jefferson County—Jefferson North Unit (Imperial)

GERMAN APPLE CAKE

2 eggs
½ to 1 cup English walnuts
2 cups sifted flour
2 cups sugar
2 teaspoons cinnamon
4 cups apples, thinly sliced and peeled
1 teaspoon baking soda
1 teaspoon vanilla extract
½ teaspoon salt
1 cup vegetable oil
Whipped topping or ice cream (optional)

Mix all ingredients together with a spoon; do not use mixer or blender. Batter will be stiff. Spread into greased and floured 9-x-13-inch pan. Bake at 350 degrees for 45 to 60 minutes. Serve with whipped topping or ice cream.

Betty Arnold
St. Genevieve County (St. Genevieve)

FRESH APPLE CAKE

1½ cups vegetable oil
2 cups sugar
2 eggs
2½ cups all-purpose flour
2 teaspoons baking powder
1 teaspoon baking soda
1 teaspoon salt
1 teaspoon vanilla extract
3 cups chopped raw apples
1 cup chopped nuts, optional

Measure oil into large mixing bowl. Add sugar and eggs and beat until creamy. Combine flour, salt, soda and baking powder. Add these dry ingredients in small amounts, beating well after each addition. Add vanilla. Fold in apples and nuts. Bake in greased and floured 9-x-13-inch pan. Bake at 350 degrees for 55 to 60 minutes. *This is very good served warm or cooled and topped with whipped topping.*

Mrs. Bill Shults (Elizabeth)
Lewis County (Ewing)

CHOPPED APPLE CAKE

4 cups apples, peeled and diced
2 cups sugar
2 eggs, well beaten
1 cup vegetable oil
1 cup nuts
2 cups all-purpose flour, sifted
1 teaspoon baking soda
1 teaspoon salt
2 teaspoons cinnamon

Mix diced apples with sugar in a large mixing bowl. Add eggs, 1 at a time, stirring after each, oil and nuts; mix well. Stir flour, soda, salt and cinnamon into batter. Pour into greased and floured 9-x-12-inch baking dish. Bake at 350 degrees 45 to 60 minutes. Let cool before frosting.

Frosting:
1 (8-ounce) package cream cheese
½ cup margarine
1 package powdered sugar (1 pound)
1 teaspoon vanilla extract

Cream cream cheese and margarine well. Stir in sugar and vanilla until very smooth. Spread on cooled cake. *Yield: 16 to 20 servings. May be kept for several days; also freezes well.*

Mrs. Morgan Harris
Clinton County (Plattsburg)

NUT CAKE

6 large eggs, separated
¾ cup sugar
1½ cups ground walnuts or pecans (use grinder, not blender)
3 tablespoons fine dry breadcrumbs

Beat egg yolks; add sugar; beat until light. Beat egg whites until stiff; fold yolks and nuts alternately into whites, then fold in crumbs. Divide dough into 2 layer cake pans that have been liberally oiled and floured. Bake at 350 degrees for 15 to 20 minutes. When cool; fill and frost.

Chocolate frosting:
½ cup sweet butter (no substitute)
½ cup sugar
2 eggs
4 ounces semi-sweet chocolate, melted and cooled
1 tablespoon instant coffee

Cream butter and sugar, add remaining ingredients. Cool and spread between layers and on top and sides of cake. *Yield: 10 to 12 servings. Finely ground nuts are used in place of flour in this traditional Viennese recipe.*

Mrs. Don Reynolds (Anneliese)
Chariton County (Salisbury)

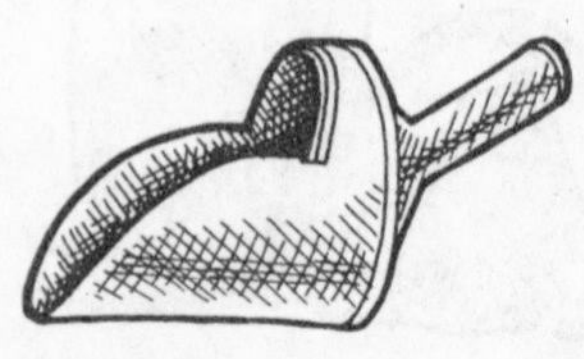

CRAZY CAKE

3 cups all-purpose flour
2 cups sugar
½ cup cocoa
1 teaspoon salt
1 teaspoon soda
1 teaspoon vanilla
2 tablespoons vinegar
¾ cup vegetable oil
2 cups cold water

Sift flour with sugar, cocoa, salt and soda. Put sifted dry ingredients in greased 12-x-8-inch baking pan. Combine remaining ingredients in mixing bowl. Blend well and pour over dry ingredients. Mix well. Bake at 350 degrees for 30 to 35 minutes. While cake is baking, make icing.

Icing:
½ cup margarine
4 tablespoons cocoa
5 tablespoons milk
1 teaspoon vanilla
1 pound powdered sugar

Combine margarine with cocoa and milk in saucepan. Bring to a boil. Remove from heat and add vanilla and powdered sugar. Beat until smooth. Spread on cake as soon as cake comes from oven. *You may add 1 cup nuts to icing, if desired.*

Flossie E. Roundtree
Cedar Unit (El Dorado Springs)

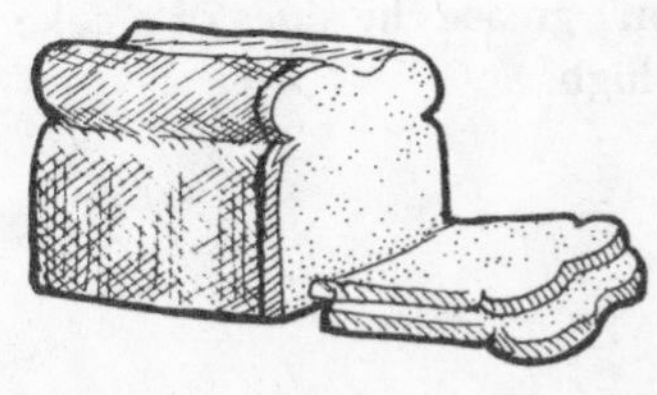

ORANGE SLICE CAKE

1 cup margarine
2 cups sugar
4 eggs
1 teaspoon baking soda
½ cup buttermilk
½ teaspoon salt
3½ cups flour
1 cup chopped dates
2 cups chopped nuts
1 pound orange slices, sliced thin
1 cup coconut
1 cup orange juice
2 cups powdered sugar

Cream margarine and sugar until smooth; add eggs, 1 at a time, beating well after each. Dissolve soda in buttermilk and add to mix. Add salt. Put flour in large bowl, add dates, nuts and orange slices; stir to coat well. Add flour mixture and coconut to creamed mixture; makes a stiff batter. Bake in greased and floured tube pan at 300 degrees for 2 hours. Remove from oven and leave in pan. Combine orange juice and powdered sugar, pour over hot cake; let set overnight. *My family prefers this cake as a Christmas goody rather than a fruit cake. It keeps as well as fruit cake and freezes beautifully.*

Laura Sullivan
Webster County (Niangua)

Don't grease the sides of a cake pan. The cake won't rise as high.

CARAMEL ICING

1 cup brown sugar, firmly packed
3 tablespoons vegetable shortening
2 tablespoons butter
¼ teaspoon salt
¼ cup milk
1½ cups powdered sugar, sifted

Combine brown sugar, shortening, butter and salt in saucepan. Bring to a boil, stirring constantly. Lower heat, add milk, and cook 3 minutes, stirring frequently. Cool and add powdered sugar. Beat until smooth. If icing is too thick, beat in a small amount of cream. Yield: Enough for top and sides of 2-layer cake. *This icing will stay moist.*

Mabel Janssens
Cedar County (El Dorado Springs)

SOUR CREAM BANANA CAKE

2 mashed bananas
2 eggs, unbeaten
½ teaspoon salt
1 cup sugar
1 cup sour cream
1 teaspoon vanilla extract
Chopped nuts, if desired
2 cups sifted flour
2 teaspoons baking powder
1 teaspoon baking soda
Dash of salt

Mash bananas until no lumps remain, then add eggs and mix well. Beat in salt, sugar, sour cream and vanilla; stir in nuts. Sift flour, baking powder, soda and dash of salt. Blend into batter. Bake in 8-inch square pan or 13-x-9-x-2-inch baking dish for 35 to 45 minutes at 325 degrees. *Frost as desired. This favorite recipe may be served as cake or bread.*

Mrs. Clyde Moore
Jackson County—Blue Springs Unit (Oak Grove)

Pies

GOOSEBERRY PIE

⅔ cup water, divided
2 cups sugar
1½ quarts fresh gooseberries
¼ cup cornstarch
1 pastry shell

Cook ⅓ cup water and sugar in saucepan over low heat 2 to 3 minutes. Add berries. Simmer gently about 5 minutes, until cooked but still whole. Using small strainer, remove berries from the syrup and place in the pastry shell. Dissolve cornstarch in remaining ⅓ cup water. Stir into syrup. Cook over moderate heat until thick and clear, stirring constantly about 3 minutes. Cool to lukewarm. Pour over berries in shell. Arrange diamond shaped pastry in pattern over the top; to serve, cut into wedges with a diamond centering each. *Serve with whipped cream or ice cream, if desired.*

For pastry:
1½ cups sifted flour
1 tablespoon sugar
⅔ cup butter or shortening
2 teaspoons almond extract
2 or 3 tablespoons water

Mix flour and sugar; cut in butter until mixture resembles coarse meal. Sprinkle almond flavoring then water over mixture, 1 tablespoon at a time, tossing quickly with a fork until dough forms a ball. Form dough into a smooth ball between palms of hands. Chill 30 minutes. Bake as other pastry shells, except after rolling out the second pastry, cut it into diamond shapes and bake on a cookie sheet.

Mrs. Claude A. Bradley
Bates County (Rich Hill)

PUMPKIN OR SQUASH PIE

2 eggs
½ cup brown sugar
½ cup granulated sugar
½ teaspoon salt
1½ teaspoons cinnamon
1½ teaspoons allspice
½ cup cream or canned milk
½ cup milk
1 cup pumpkin or squash
1 (8 or 9-inch) pastry shell

Combine eggs, sugars and salt and beat until smooth. Then add spices, cream, milk and pumpkin or squash. Mix together well and pour into prepared pastry shell. Bake at 375 to 400 degrees for 45 minutes to 1 hour.

Martha McClintock
Nodaway County (Maryville)

FRESH CONCORD GRAPE PIE

1¾ pounds Concord grapes
2 tablespoons light corn syrup
1 cup sugar
1½ tablespoons cornstarch
Pinch of salt
1 teaspoon lemon juice
1 double crust pastry

Wash the grapes, stem and separate skin from pulp. Place pulp in a saucepan and simmer for 5 minutes. Strain through a coarse strainer to remove seeds. Return strained pulp to the saucepan and heat to boiling. Mix syrup, cornstarch, sugar and salt and add to pulp, stirring briskly. Simmer 5 minutes and cool. Add grape skins and lemon juice. Pour into unbaked pastry shell. Place a lattice of pastry over the top or a full crust if desired. Brush with milk or cream and sprinkle lightly with sugar. Bake at 375 degrees for 40 to 45 minutes or until crust is brown and crisp.

Miss Hulling's Bakeries
St. Louis County-Central Metro Unit (St. Louis)

DAIQUIRI PIE

1 (4-serving) package lemon pudding and pie filling
1 (3-ounce) package lime gelatin
⅓ cup sugar
2½ cups water, divided
2 eggs, slightly beaten
½ cup light Bacardi rum
1¾ cup thawed whipped topping
1 baked (9-inch) graham cracker pie shell, cooled

Combine pudding mix, gelatin and sugar in saucepan. Stir in ½ cup water and beaten eggs; blend well. Add remaining water. Cook over medium heat, stirring constantly, until mixture comes to a full boil. Remove from heat; stir in rum. Chill. Thoroughly blend in whipped topping into chilled mixture. Spoon into pie shell and chill until firm, about 2 hours. *Garnish with additional whipped topping and lime slices if desired.*

Mrs. Leonard Hadasek (Maxine)
Jasper County (Joplin)

PECAN PIE

3 eggs
1 cup sugar
½ cup white corn syrup
¼ cup butter, melted
1 cup pecans
1 (9-inch) pie shell

Beat eggs well. Gradually add sugar. Beat until thick. Add corn syrup and butter. Blend well. Stir in pecans. Pour into baked pie shell. Bake at 375 degrees for 45 minutes to 1 hour.

Flossie E. Rountree
Cedar Unit (El Dorado Springs)

TRANSPARENT PIE

3 eggs, separated
3 tablespoons water, divided
1 cup sugar
2 tablespoons flour
½ cup margarine
1 teaspoon vanilla extract
1 (8-inch) pastry shell, unbaked

Separate eggs, beat yolks with 1 tablespoon water and set aside. Blend sugar and flour, set aside. Melt margarine in heavy pan over low heat. Add sugar, flour, 2 tablespoons water and stir constantly until all sugar is melted and mixture is creamy. Remove from heat; add egg yolks, return to heat and stir until well blended. Add vanilla. Pour into pastry shell. Bake at 375 degrees for 30 minutes. Remove from oven.

Meringue:
Beat egg whites until very stiff; add 6 tablespoons sugar, 1 at a time, beating after each addition. Bake at 425 degrees for 5 to 7 minutes. *This was my father's favorite pie. The recipe was passed down from the Miller family.*

Mrs. Harold Gamble
Clinton County (Plattsburg)

EASY PIE CRUST

1 cup flour
2 tablespoons powdered sugar
½ cup margarine less 1 tablespoon, softened

Place flour and sugar in pie pan. Mix in margarine until mixture is crumbly. Press onto bottom and sides of pan. Bake at 350 degrees for 15 minutes. *Makes 1 pie crust. Fill with no-bake filling. This is fast and easy for busy people.*

June Williams
Reynolds County (Ellington)

ANGEL CHIFFON PIE

1 envelope unflavored gelatin
½ cup water
¼ cup light or dark rum
1½ cups prepared mincemeat
3 egg whites
⅓ cup sugar
⅛ teaspoon salt
1 cup heavy cream, whipped
1 (9-inch) baked pastry shell

Sprinkle unflavored gelatin on water in saucepan. Place over low heat; stir constantly until gelatin is dissolved. Remove from heat. Stir in rum and mincemeat. Chill until mixture mounds slightly when dropped from spoon. Beat egg whites until stiff, but not dry. Gradually add sugar and salt and beat until very stiff. Fold in gelatin mixture. Fold in whipped cream. Turn into pastry shell. Chill until firm. Garnish with additional whipped cream and sprinkle with nutmeg. *The additional whipped cream is really not necessary. This makes a light airy pie with the flavor of mincemeat but not the heavy traditional texture.*

Ramona Kitchen
Oregon County (Alton)

RAISIN CREAM PIE

2 or 3 eggs, separated
1 tablespoon flour
1 tablespoon cornstarch
1 cup sugar
¼ teaspoon salt
1 teaspoon cinnamon
2 cups milk
¾ cup uncooked raisins
Baked (9-inch) pastry shell

Mix all ingredients together except raisins. Beat until smooth. Add raisins, bring to a rolling boil, stirring constantly. Cool slightly. Pour into pastry shell. Top with meringue and bake at 350 degrees until brown, about 20 minutes.

Raisin Cream Pie (continued)

Meringue:

2 or 3 egg whites (from above)
1 teaspoon vanilla extract
1 tablespoon sugar

Beat egg whites until stiff; add vanilla and sugar. Beat mixture until bowl can be turned upside down and egg whites remain in bowl. Spread over pie. *Pie variations: omit cinnamon and raisins and add 3 tablespoons cocoa for chocolate pie. Omit cinnamon and raisins and add 1 teaspoon banana extract and sliced bananas to shell.*

Jennie Vertrees
Mercer County (Princeton)

PECAN PIE

½ cup sugar
¾ cup light corn syrup
3 eggs, beaten separately
Dash of salt
1 teaspoon vanilla extract
2 tablespoons melted butter
¾ cup pecans

Mix sugar and syrup together. Add beaten eggs, salt and vanilla. Add butter. Pour into an unbaked pastry shell. Place pecans on top of pie. Bake at 325 degrees for 30 to 45 minutes. *My mother, Ina Geery Brown (1881-1956) loved to bake and share her pecan pies with relatives and friends. Her great grandparents, Charles and Margaret Kerr Scanland, of Virginia, were early pioneers to Missouri, locating near Frankford in Pike County. I am a member of the sixth generation of John Fielding Scanland of Virginia who served in the Revolution in 1777.*

Orpha B. Waddell
Pike County

Desserts

FROZEN CHOCOLATE CHARLOTTE

2 packages lady fingers, 12 inches each
¼ cup white cream de menthe or rum
2 (8-ounce) packages semi-sweet chocolate squares
3 tablespoons instant coffee
½ cup boiling water
6 eggs, separated
½ cup sugar
1 teaspoon vanilla extract
1½ cups heavy cream whipped or whipped topping

Split lady fingers, but do not separate into individual pieces. Brush flat surface with cream de menthe or rum. Line sides of a 9-inch spring form pan with lady fingers, 1 rounded side against pan. Separate remaining lady fingers; line bottom of pan, overlapping to fit. Melt chocolate in double boiler over hot, not boiling, water, stirring occasionally. Dissolve coffee in boiling water. Beat egg yolks in small bowl at high speed until foamy. Beat in sugar gradually; continue beating until thick. Reduce speed, beat in vanilla, coffee and melted chocolate. Wash beaters. Beat egg whites in large bowl until stiff. Stir about 1 cup egg whites into chocolate to lighten it. Fold chocolate mixture into remaining egg whites. Fold in whipped cream. Pour into lined pan. Freeze until firm. Garnish with chocolate curls and piped rosettes of whipped cream, if desired. Cover with foil. Refreeze. *Keeps well up to 1 month. To serve, remove sides of pan. Place on cake plate. Yield: 12 to 16 servings.*

Louise Gastineau
Caldwell County (Cowgill)

CHOCOLATE COCONUT DESSERT

1 (6-ounce) package semi-sweet chocolate pieces
1 (13-ounce) can evaporated milk
1 (10½-ounce) package (5 cups) miniature marshmallows
1⅓ cups flaked coconut
6 tablespoons margarine
½ teaspoon butter flavoring
2 cups rice cereal, crushed
1 cup chopped walnuts
½ to 1 gallon vanilla ice cream

In a saucepan, melt chocolate in milk. Bring to a boil; boil gently, uncovered, 4 minutes or until thick, stirring constantly. Add marshmallows; heat and stir until melted. Chill. In skillet cook and stir coconut in margarine until lightly browned. Stir in cereal, nuts and butter flavoring. Spread 3 cups of the cereal mixture in bottom of a 13-x-9-x-2-inch pan. Cut ice cream in half lengthwise and then horizontally into slices to cover pan. Arrange half the ice cream over the cereal. Spread with half the chocolate mixture. Repeat layers. Top with remaining cereal. Cover; freeze until firm. Let stand at room temperature about 10 minutes before serving. *Makes 16 servings.*

Mrs. Dale E. Grubb
Atchison County (Fairfax)

To prevent pie crusts from becoming soggy, brush pre-baked crust with lightly beaten egg white immediately after baking. When completely cooled, fill as usual.

STRAWBERRY SURPRISE DESSERT

3 cups large pretzels, coarsely broken
¾ cup margarine, melted
3 tablespoons sugar
1 (8-ounce) package cream cheese, softened
1 egg, slightly beaten
1 cup powdered sugar, sifted
1 teaspoon vanilla
1 (8-ounce) carton Cool Whip
1 (6-ounce) package strawberry-flavored gelatin
2 cups boiling water
2 (10-ounce) packages frozen strawberries

Combine pretzels with margarine and sugar. Spread evenly in 13-x-9-inch baking pan. Bake at 350 for 5 minutes. Cool. Combine cream cheese with egg, powdered sugar, vanilla and Cool Whip. Blend thoroughly. Pour over pretzels. Dissolve gelatin in boiling water. Stir in frozen strawberries. Stir until strawberries are thoroughly combined with gelatin. Cool until syrupy. Pour over Cool Whip mixture. Refrigerate overnight.

Mrs. Paul Ensor
Monroe County (Holliday)

Always chill the beaters of your mixer as well as the bowl you will use to whip cream.

FROZEN PINK DELIGHT

1 (8-ounce) package cream cheese
¾ cup sugar
1 (20-ounce) can crushed pineapple, drained
1 (10-ounce) package frozen strawberries with juice
2 sliced bananas
1 (8-ounce) carton whipped topping

Soften and blend cream cheese with sugar. Mix together the drained pineapple, strawberries, bananas, and whipped topping. Combine the cream cheese mixture with the fruit and whipped topping mixture. Pour into a 10-inch bundt pan and freeze until firm. Cover with aluminum foil. When ready to serve, unmold by placing in warm water a few seconds before inverting onto a serving plate. Slice and serve. Any leftover portion can be returned to the freezer. *Yield: 10 to 12 servings. This is delicious served any time of the year, especially because it can be prepared ahead of time.*

Mrs. Larry Lumley (Karen)
Knox County (Novelty)

PUMPKIN DESSERT

3 cups sugar
1 cup vegetable oil
3 eggs
2 cups canned pumpkin
3 cups flour
½ teaspoon salt
½ teaspoon baking powder
1 teaspoon baking soda
1 teaspoon cloves
1 teaspoon cinnamon
1 teaspoon nutmeg

Beat sugar and oil thoroughly; add eggs and pumpkin; add dry ingredients that have been sifted together; beat until batter is smooth. Put into 2 loaf pans or a tube pan. Bake at 350 degrees for 45 minutes for bread (serve with butter) or bake for 1¼ hours for cake (serve with whipped cream).

Joanne Propst
Iron County (Ironton)

BANANA SPLIT DESSERT

1½ cups butter, divided
2 cups crushed graham crackers
2 eggs
2 cups powdered sugar
3 to 5 bananas, sliced
1 (20-ounce) can crushed pineapple, drained
1 (12-ounce) carton whipped topping
½ cup maraschino cherries
¾ cup chopped nuts

Mix ½ cup melted butter and cracker crumbs; pat into a 9-x-13-inch pan; set aside. Beat egg, 1 cup butter and sugar together at least 15 minutes; spread evenly over crust. Distribute sliced bananas over the filling. Add the crushed pineapple; top with whipped topping. Garnish with cherries and nuts. Chill 6 to 8 hours before serving. *Serves 16. This makes a good dessert when serving men. They love it!*

Mrs. Ethel Thomas
Saline County (Sweet Springs)

CHERRY JUBILEE

1½ cups graham cracker crumbs
¼ cup sugar
½ cup melted margarine
1 (8-ounce) package softened cream cheese
1 package Dream Whip
1 can cherry pie filling

Mix cracker crumbs, sugar and margarine; press into bottom of 9-x-13-inch pan. Soften cream cheese; mix Dream Whip according to package directions; combine the 2 ingredients. Spread on crust in pan. Top with pie filling. *This is very rich and delicious, always a special dessert on holidays.*

Helen B. Thompson
Shannon County (Birch Tree)

FANTASTIC FOUR LAYER DESSERT

Layer 1:

1 cup flour
½ cup butter or margarine, melted
½ cup chopped pecans
½ cup powdered sugar

Combine all ingredients; press into bottom of 10-inch baking dish. Bake at 350 degrees for 12 to 15 minutes or until golden brown. Cool.

Layer 2:

1 (8-ounce) package cream cheese, at room temperature
1 cup whipped topping
1 cup powdered sugar

Mix ingredients with electric mixer until smooth; spread over layer 1.

Layer 3:

1 (3-ounce) package vanilla instant pudding
1 (3-ounce) package chocolate instant pudding
1 teaspoon vanilla extract
3 cups milk

Beat ingredients on lowest speed of electric mixer for 2 minutes; spread over layer 2.

Layer 4:

½ cup whipped topping

Spread over layer 3. Sprinkle chocolate shavings over top for garnish. Refrigerate. Let set at least 1 hour before serving. *Yield: 6 to 8 servings. This recipe is a favorite with my guests. The extra effort is rewarding . . . it's fantastic!*

Mrs. Lawrence Sutherland (Joanne)
Jackson County—Independence Unit (Independence)

Puddings

BLACKBERRY PUDDING

2 eggs
1 cup sugar
1 teaspoon baking soda
1 tablespoon buttermilk
1 cup blackberry juice
1 cup flour

Mix all ingredients together and pour into a 9-inch square pan. Bake at 350 degrees for 25 to 30 minutes.

Sauce:

2 cups milk
3 tablespoons flour or cornstarch
1½ cups sugar
2 tablespoons butter
1 teaspoon vanilla extract

Place all sauce ingredients except vanilla in a saucepan and cook over moderate heat until mixture thickens. Remove and add vanilla. Spoon sauce over pudding when it is served. *This recipe is an old family recipe given to me by my mother-in-law, Mrs. Ruby Robertson.*

Kay Robertson
Wright County (Mountain Grove)

PEACH PUDDING DESSERT

1 cup self-rising flour
¾ cup sugar
½ cup milk
3 tablespoons vegetable oil
1 large can sliced peaches, drained
1 cup brown sugar
¼ cup chopped nuts
1 teaspoon cinnamon
1 cup boiling water

Mix flour and sugar, beat in milk and oil until smooth. Pour in ungreased 8-x-8-x-2-inch pan. Arrange peaches on top, mix brown sugar, nuts and cinnamon, sprinkle over top of peaches. Pour boiling water over top. Bake at 350 degrees about 60 minutes, or until wooden pick comes out clean. Serve with whipped topping, if desired.

Mrs. Steve Carlisle (Donna)
Dallas County (Louisburg)

LEMON BISQUE ICEBOX PUDDING

1 can evaporated milk
1¼ cups boiling water
1 package lemon gelatin
½ cup sugar
3 tablespoons lemon juice
⅛ teaspoon salt
2½ cups wafer or graham cracker crumbs

Chill milk. Dissolve gelatin in water; add sugar, lemon juice and salt. When congealed slightly, whip gelatin. Beat milk and combine. Spread half of crumbs in pan; pour mixture over crumbs; sprinkle remaining half of crumbs on top. Serve plain or with whipped cream. *Approximately 12 servings.*

Kitty Parker
Shelby County (Shelbyville)

PETER PAN PUDDING

14 graham crackers, crushed
¼ cup butter or margarine, melted
¾ cup sugar, divided
1 package unflavored gelatin
2 tablespoons pineapple juice
1 cup boiling water
1 large can Milnot milk
1 cup crushed pineapple
1 cup shredded coconut
½ cup chopped nuts
24 marshamallows, cut up
1 package strawberry gelatin

Combine graham crackers, butter and ¼ cup sugar. Press into a 14-x-11-x-3-inch pan. Dissolve unflavored gelatin in pineapple juice. Add boiling water and let stand until it starts to congeal. Whip Milnot and add ½ cup sugar, gelatin, pineapple, coconut, nuts, and marshmallows. Pour mixture over the graham cracker crust and place in refrigerator until well set. Then pour slightly congealed strawberry gelatin over top, return to refrigerator; chill until firm. *Makes 12 large servings. Better when made the day before.*

Mrs. J. H. Smith (Betty)
Lewis County (Durham)

PERSIMMON PUDDING

1 cup ripe persimmon pulp
¼ cup brown sugar
¾ cup white flour
½ cup whole wheat flour
1 teaspoon baking soda
¼ teaspoon salt
1 cup milk
1 cup walnuts, chopped
½ cup raisins
½ cup dates, chopped

Mix persimmon pulp with sugar. Add flours, soda and salt alternately with milk. Stir in nuts, raisins and dates. Place in baking dish or oiled individual molds set in a pan of water. Bake at 350 degrees for 1½ hours. Serve with lemon sauce or your favorite sauce. *If desired, ¼ teaspoon cinnamon may be added to batter.*

Alberta Bennage
Lawrence County (Marionville)

Variation: Run persimmons through colander with milk and water. Set aside and add to batter last. *This recipe is a special addition to a Thanksgiving or Christmas dinner. It has become a tradition in our family on both occasions. If persimmons aren't available at your supermarket, may I suggest you take a country outing, locate a persimmon tree and pick your own. Just be certain they are ripe!*

Mrs. Aubrey Schlotzhauer
Cooper County (Pilot Grove)

DATE PUDDING

1 cup flour
1 cup sugar
½ cup milk
1 cup chopped dates
1 cup chopped nuts
2 teaspoons baking powder
1 cup brown sugar
2 cups boiling water
½ cup butter or margarine

Mix flour, sugar, milk, dates, nuts and baking powder and pour in an ungreased 9-x-13-inch pan. Cover with brown sugar, boiling water and butter. Bake at 350 degrees for 20 minutes or until done. Cool and serve with whipped topping. *Yield: 16 servings.*

Mrs. Murrell Misner
Daviess County (Gallatin)

Ice Cream

ICE CREAM

2 quarts milk
5 or 6 eggs, beaten
2½ cups sugar
½ teaspoon salt
1 can sweetened condensed milk
3 tablespoons vanilla extract
6 junket tablets

Boil the milk, eggs, sugar and salt until thick. Then cool completely. When ready to freeze, pour mixture into ice cream freezer and add the condensed milk, vanilla and junket tablets, which have been dissolved in water. Finish filling freezer with whole milk to freezer line. For richer ice cream, use canned milk instead of whole. Freeze until thick. *Makes 3 quarts.*

Martha McClintock
Nodaway County (Maryville)

BUTTER PECAN ICE CREAM

4 eggs
2 cups granulated sugar
2 (3⅝-ounce) packages butter pecan instant pudding mix
1 (8-ounce) package frozen whipped topping
½ cup pecans, chopped
1 teaspoon vanilla extract
½ gallon whole milk

Beat eggs. Add remaining ingredients, except milk. Beat with electric mixer until thoroughly blended. Pour into ice cream freezer. Add milk. Freeze according to manufacturer's directions. *Strawberries, walnuts, et cetera can be substituted for pecans. Use corresponding instant pudding mix.*

Mrs. Anna Mae Dickerson
Ripley County (Doniphan)

THE FIVE THREE'S
(Frozen Sherbet)

3 cups water
3 cups sugar
Juice of 3 oranges
Juice of 3 lemons
3 bananas (mashed)

Mix and freeze. When half frozen, remove from freezer and whip for smoothness. Return to freezer and keep until serving time.

Mrs. Chester Parker
Pulaski County (Waynesville)

"NOAH'S ARK" COVERED BRIDGE

This bridge was originally built in 1878 by the farmers of the area who realized the need for it. Standing one mile southeast of Platte City, the bridge spanned the Little Platte River.

The bridge was constructed of hand-hewn lumber cut from nearby oak trees and hauled to the bridge location by oxen teams. The strong arch of the bridge shows the ingenuity of the pioneer builders. It derives its name from Judge Noah Berry, county court judge at the time of construction.

The original bridge stood until July, 1965, when a flood collapsed the bridge and washed it several miles downstream. At that time a decision was made to reconstruct the bridge on the Platte County Fairgrounds in Platte City, where it now stands.

Gifts from the Kitchen and Potpourri

Gifts from the Kitchen

BARBECUE SAUCE

½ cup prepared mustard
¼ cup Kitchen Bouquet
1 teaspoon pepper
1 teaspoon garlic salt
1 teaspoon steak sauce
1 teaspoon Worcestershire sauce
½ cup prepared barbecue sauce

Mix all ingredients together. Blend well. This can be used on beef, pork or chicken. Brush on all sides of meat as you barbecue it.

Claudia Jensen
Newton Unit (Neosho)

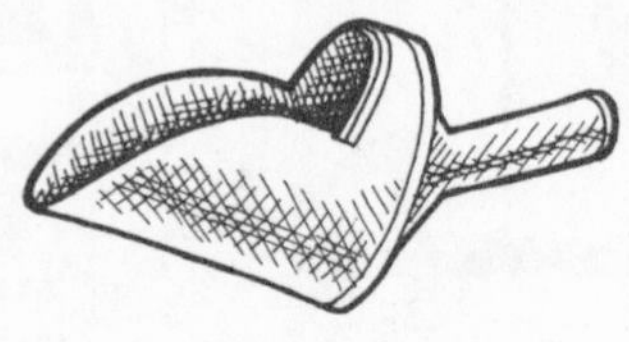

FRESH PICKLES

7 cups cucumbers, sliced
1 cup onions, sliced
2 cups red or green sweet peppers, finely chopped
1 tablespoon celery seed
2 cups sugar
1 cup vinegar
1 tablespoon salt

Combine all ingredients. Refrigerate. Keeps 7 weeks, or you may add fresh cucumbers as available and keep it going all summer.

Clarin Beaman
Polk County (Bolivar)

CORN COB JELLY

14 large red corn cobs to make 3 cups cob juice
3 cups sugar
1 package Sure-jel

Wash corn cobs well. Cut both ends off cobs to be sure there are no insects in cobs. Place cobs in large container and cover completely with water. Boil 30 minutes. Remove cobs and strain juice through heavy cloth. Mix 3 cups juice and 1 package Sure-jel. Boil, then add sugar and cook according to pectin package directions.

Mrs. Alfred McKemy
Ray County (Hardin)

HARVEST CORN

2 quarts popped popcorn
1 can mixed nuts
1 large can shoestring potatoes
⅓ cup melted butter
1 teaspoon lemon pepper
1 teaspoon dill weed
1 teaspoon Worcestershire sauce
½ teaspoon garlic powder
¼ teaspoon salt

Mix popcorn, nuts and potatoes on a 15-x-10-x-1-inch sheet cake pan. Melt butter and mix in next 5 ingredients. Pour over popcorn mixture. Bake at 350 degrees for 5 to 6 minutes. *Yield: 10 servings.*

Mrs. Ruth Brandt
Knox County (Edina)

CARAMEL POPCORN

- **2 cups brown sugar, firmly packed**
- **½ pound margarine**
- **½ cup light corn syrup**
- **1 teaspoon salt**
- **½ teaspoon soda**
- **8 quarts popped popcorn**

Combine brown sugar, margarine, corn syrup and salt in saucepan. Bring to a boil. Cook over low heat, stirring constantly, for 5 minutes. Stir in soda. Pour over popcorn in large roasting pan. Bake at 250 degrees for 1 hour, stirring every 15 minutes.

Reta Shellhart
Benton County (Cole Camp)

ZESTY FIESTA CORN

- **½ envelope (about 2 tablespoons) taco seasoning mix**
- **¼ cup water**
- **¼ cup vegetable oil**
- **¼ cup vinegar**
- **1 (16-ounce) can whole kernel corn, drained**
- **2 medium tomatoes, peeled and diced (about 1½ cups)**
- **½ cup sliced ripe olives**
- **¼ cup diced green pepper**

In a large bowl, stir together seasoning mix and water until blended. Add oil and vinegar. Add corn, diced tomatoes, olives and green pepper; toss lightly. Chill several hours or overnight, stirring mixture occasionally. *Serves 6 to 8. Serve cold.*

Mrs. Ralph Brown (Carryl)
Ozark County (Gainesville)

HOT FRUIT CASSEROLE

1 (15½-ounce) can pineapple chunks, drained
1 (16-ounce) can peach slices, drained
1 (16-ounce) jar spiced apple rings, drained
1 (16-ounce) can pear halves, drained
1 (16-ounce) can apricot halves, drained
2 tablespoons all-purpose flour
½ cup brown sugar, firmly packed
½ cup butter or margarine
1 cup dry cocktail sherry

Arrange drained fruit in layers in deep baking dish. Combine remaining ingredients in saucepan. Cook over low heat, stirring constantly, until mixture has thickened. Pour over fruit. Refrigerate overnight. Before serving, bake at 350 degrees for 30 to 45 minutes, until hot and bubbly. *Keeps well in refrigerator and may be reheated.*

Mrs. J. Loren Washburn (Anita)
Morgan County (Versailles)

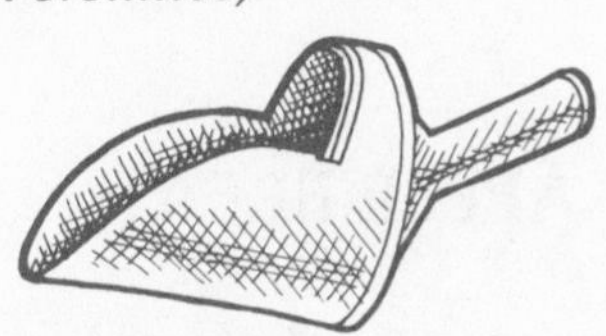

PARTY MINTS

1 (8-ounce) package cream cheese
2 pounds powdered sugar
½ teaspoon mint flavoring
Granulated sugar

Combine cream cheese, powdered sugar and flavoring, using hands to knead in powdered sugar. Make into small balls and roll in granulated sugar and let dry overnight. *These may be pressed into mint molds for variety of shapes. Food coloring may also be added for variety.*

Judy Kennedy
Hickory County (Wheatland)

BANANA BREAD

¾ cup sugar
½ cup butter
1 egg
½ teaspoon salt
1 cup mashed ripe bananas
2 cups flour
1 teaspoon baking soda
1 cup black walnuts, cut fine or ½ teaspoon walnut flavoring

Beat the sugar, butter and egg together with the salt. Add the bananas. Sift the flour and soda together and add to the other mixture. Add the walnuts or the flavoring. Bake in a loaf pan at 325 degrees for 1 to 1½ hours. *This recipe was given to my mother by a well-known Kansas City pediatrician, Dr. Harry Gilkey, at least 45 years ago.*

Carolyn Weir
Jackson County—Independence Unit (Independence)

APPLE BREAD

2 eggs
½ cup melted butter
1 cup sugar
½ cup orange juice
2 cups diced apples (or more)
1 cup chopped nuts
½ teaspoon salt
1 teaspoon vanilla extract
2 cups flour
1 teaspoon baking soda

Mix all ingredients well, and pour into a 9-x-4-inch greased bread pan. Sprinkle top with a mixture of sugar and cinnamon, and bake at 350 degrees for 1 hour and 10 minutes. *This makes a nice gift, wrapped in foil or plastic wrap. Sometimes I divide the recipe, make 2, and cut baking time.*

Mrs. Wilburn Bushnell (Loy)
St. Louis County—North County Unit (Florissant)

APPLE ROLL

3 cups thinly sliced apples
1 cup water
1½ cups plus 2 tablespoons sugar, divided
2 cups all-purpose flour
1 teaspoon salt
4 teaspoons baking powder
¾ cup shortening
About ¾ cup milk
½ teaspoon cinnamon
Butter

Prepare apples. Bring water and 1 cup sugar to a boil; keep hot until ready to use. Combine flour, 2 tablespoons sugar, salt, baking powder and shortening until mixture is crumbly. Add enough milk to make soft dough; stir with fork until all flour disappears. Knead as with biscuit dough, roll into an oblong piece, ¼-inch thick. Cover with sliced apples, roll dough over apples, jelly roll style. Slice into 1-inch thick pieces and place in 8-inch pan. Pour hot syrup over slices; sprinkle with mixture of ½ cup sugar and cinnamon; dot with butter. Bake at 350 degrees 30 to 35 minutes until golden brown. Cool in pan. Very good served plain or with ice cream. This is a favorite dessert for a carry-in dinner.

Mrs. Emmitt Holton (Helen)
Scotland County (Memphis)

OATMEAL BREAD

1 package yeast
¼ cup warm water
1 tablespoon sugar
4½ to 5 cups flour, divided
1 cup quick cool oatmeal
⅓ cup brown sugar
½ cup molasses
¼ cup shortening
1 teaspoon salt
1 cup water
1 cup milk

Dissolve yeast and sugar in warm water; set aside. Combine oatmeal, brown sugar, molasses, shortening and salt. Combine water and milk and bring to a boil; pour over oatmeal mixture and let cool. Add yeast and 1 cup flour. Wait until bubbles come to the top, then add 3½ to 4 cups flour. Let rise, knead and make into 2 loaves. Let rise again. Bake at 350 degrees about 45 minutes or until golden brown. *This is an old family recipe given to me by my husband's aunt, and is a favorite of my children. It makes a good item for Christmas gifts and bazaars.*

Charlotte Davis
Laclede County (Lebanon)

PLATTE COUNTY PIE

2 large eggs
½ cup flour
1 cup sugar
¼ melted butter or margarine
1 teaspoon vanilla
1 cup chopped walnuts
1 cup chocolate chips
1 unbaked 9" pie shell

Beat eggs. Add flour and sugar and continue beating. Add melted butter and allow to cool. Add vanilla to cooled mixture. Add walnuts and chocolate chips. Pour into pie shell. Bake at 325 for 1 hour.

Optional: Top with whipped cream.

Mrs. Candy Kuebler
South Platte County (Parkville)

BROWN SUGAR COOKIES WITH FUDGE ICING

Cookies:

1⅔ cups brown sugar, firmly packed
⅔ cup butter or margarine, softened
2 eggs, beaten
2 teaspoons vanilla
1 teaspoon cream of tartar
1 teaspoon soda
¼ teaspoon salt
4 cups all-purpose flour

Cream brown sugar and butter. When light and fluffy, add eggs. Mix well. Add vanilla. Add dry ingredients. Blend well. Roll out on heavily floured board. Cut with cookie cutter. Bake at 350 degrees for 8 to 10 minutes.

Icing:

1 cup sugar
¼ cup cocoa
¼ cup butter or margarine
½ cup half-and-half
2 tablespoons white corn syrup
1 teaspoon vanilla
1½ to 2 cups powdered sugar, sifted
Dash of salt

Combine in saucepan all ingredients except powdered sugar and vanilla. Stir constantly until mixture reaches a full rolling boil. Boil 3 minutes. Remove from heat. Cool and add powdered sugar and vanilla. Beat well. Spread on cookies. *This has been a favorite cookie of my five children and their friends. It is an old recipe my great-aunt Mayme Hoppers always had for her children and grandchildren.*

Hope Chasteen
Clay County—Liberty Unit (Liberty)

LIP COOKIES

2 pounds raisins
4 cups sugar
4 cups lard
7 eggs
½ gallon molasses
3 tablespoons cinnamon
1 cup buttermilk
½ cup baking soda
3 pints nut meats
Flour

Cover raisins in large saucepan with water and boil; drain. In a very large bowl, mix sugar, lard and eggs. Blend well, then add molasses and cinnamon and mix again. Dissolve soda in buttermilk and add to other mixture with raisins and nuts. Mix in enough flour to make a dough that can be rolled. Dough may be refrigerated several days before baking. Bake on ungreased cookie sheet at 350 degrees about 10 minutes. *This makes a lard can (5 gallon) full. The longer the cookies are kept, the better they get. This recipe is over 100 years old and a family tradition.*

Bertha Smith
Livingston County (Chillicothe)

MISSOURI FRUIT CAKE

1⅔ cups light brown sugar, firmly packed
¾ cup butter
2 teaspoons soda
2 cups applesauce
3 cups all-purpose flour
1 teaspoon cinnamon
1 teaspoon allspice
1 teaspoon nutmeg
½ cup raisins
½ cup black walnuts
1 teaspoon vanilla
1 teaspoon lemon flavoring

Combine brown sugar and butter in saucepan. Cook, over low heat, stirring frequently, under butter melts. Mix soda and applesauce. Add to butter and sugar. Stir. Sift flour with cinnamon, allspice and nutmeg. Dust raisins and nuts in a little of flour mixture. Add remaining flour to applesauce mixture. Add raisins, nuts, vanilla, and lemon flavoring. Mix well. Pour into large loaf pan, the bottom of which has been lined with waxed paper. Bake at 315 degrees for 45 to 60 minutes. Cover with brown paper until ready to brown.

Icing:
4 tablespoons butter, melted
1 cup powdered sugar, sifted
2 or more tablespoons condensed milk
1 teaspoon vanilla

Blend sugar gradually into melted butter. Add condensed milk, 1 tablespoon at a time, until icing reaches desired consistency. Add vanilla. Mix well. *You may put raisins and nuts on cake. This recipe is from Kentucky. It is called "Missouri" fruitcake, because some of the ingredients had to be ordered from St. Louis.*

Shirley DeBlois
St. Louis County—South County Unit (St. Louis)

AFTERNOON TEA MENU (1903)

Bouillon
Lobster Sandwiches — Chicken Truffle Sandwiches
Lettuce Sandwiches
Salted Almonds — Olives — Bonbons — Cakes
Tea — Coffee
Chocolate, or Claret Punch

About After-Dinner Coffee: Black coffee in after-dinner coffee cups is a digestive agent — a gastronomic expletive — not a beverage. To cream it is to pervert its meaning and to defeat the end for which it is served. It is well known that the addition of cream or milk to coffee causes a chemical change in both ingredients. To some stomachs creamed coffee, or cafe au lait, is poisonous. Clear black coffee is a tonic and agrees with everybody. (1903)

Water at the Dinner Table: To toss off a glass of water as soon as one sits down to a meal is an infringement of table etiquette. Those who recognize the fact do not always bethink themselves of the reason lying back of the "fool rule." To fill the stomach with iced water is to check the process of digestion temporarily. To add to the water a plateful of hot soup is to disgust the diaphragm by a load of lukewarm liquid, very like the dish-water in the pan of an untidy scullion. (1903)

About China: Tea, coffee and chocolate are more delicious when sipped from Sevres and Limoges; our sensitive finger-tips recoil from the blunt edges of pressed glass. To set stone china and thick tumblers before a tired and hungry husband would insult one who deserves the best of everything. (1881)

One Hundred Pounds of Good Soap for $1.30: Take potash, 6 lbs., 75-; lard, 4 lbs., 50-; resin, ¼ lb., 5-.
Beat up the resin, mix all together and set aside for five days; then put the whole into a ten-gallon cask of warm water, and stir twice a day for ten days; at the expiration of which time you will have 100 pounds of excellent soap. (1881)

On Dinner: Dinner — the evening dinner in particular — gives the driven man a chance for his life. He sins against light and opportunity when he carries the bolting habit to the third meal. It may be vulgar to talk of chewing. Our very babies are taught to say "masticate," instead. It is more vulgar not to do the thing itself. (1903)

Smoking. This vice — for, carried to the extent that it now is, it is truly one — in which even boys indulge with the freedom and abandonment of men, is an evil that cannot be too severely reprobated, for it must be evident to thedullest comprehension that the constant absorption, however minute the quantity, of the fumes of a deadly drug, cannot be daily persisted in without injury to the system . . . Smokers should in all cases avoid using short or dirty pipes, as the rank oil given off from the burning tobacco, by irritating cracks or sores on the lips, very often induces a cancer of the lower lip; besides this danger, such a custom taints the breath most offensively.

(1867)

Etiquette At The Table: The napkin should not be tucked under the chin, nor spread out upon the breast.

Take plenty of time to eat; haste is vulgar.

If a servant is at hand, do not ask your neighbor to pass anything.

The napkins is for the mouth only; do not use it to wipe the face, hands or beard.

Express pleasure, if you will, when you depart, but *not for your dinner.*

Drink from the cup, not the saucer.

Never pour gravy on a plate without permission.

Bread only may be placed on the tablecloth.

It is not elegant to take a bone in the fingers for the purpose of picking it.

Ladies and gentlemen should be properly dressed at meals. Curl papers for the woman and shirt-sleeves for the man are vulgar.

Don't be vulgar, but don't show that you are trying hard not to be vulgar.

(1904)

Servants. If a butler be engaged to do the family serving and waiting, he understands his business, or he should not apply for the place. The rules written out here are for the benefit of households where but one, or at the most, two maids are kept. I assume that the waitress takes charge of the table after the mistress has once shown her how it is to be set.

By the way, I hope you call her a "maid", not a "girl". The latter word has been so rubbed and soiled by persistent usage on the part of domesticated foreigners, who shed the name of "servant" as soon as they stamp upon American soil, and by the handling of would-be "genteel" housewives, that people of refinement hesitate to touch it. What the old-fashioned New Englanders called "hired help" would shake the dust off the soles of the shoes they are not quite used to wearing, were you to allude to them as servants. "Maid" sounds well, bearing to their tickled ears a certain dignity not unsuited to their new estate.

(1903)

Tablesetting — Silverware. Never allow your servants to put wiped knives on your table, for, generally speaking, you may see that they have been wiped with a dirty cloth. If a knife is brightly cleaned, they are compelled to use a clean cloth. (1867)

To Take Stains of Wine out of Linen. Hold the articles in milk while it is boiling on the fire, and the stains will soon disappear. (1867)

Wine. It is surprising now-a-days, the quantity of wine some few young single ladies at parties can imbibe without being intoxicated; but whether, if such ladies marry, they will make "fruitful vines", is quite another matter; but of this I am quite sure, that such girls will, as a rule, make delicate, hysterical and unhealthy wives. The young are peculiarly sensitive to the evil effects of overstimulation. Excessive wine-drinking with them is a canker eating into their very lives. Time it is that these facts were proclaimed through the length and breadth of our land before mischief be done past remedy. (1887)

Champagne at Parties. The champagne cup is one of the most fascinating but most desperately dangerous and deceptive drinks a young girl can imbibe and should be shunned as the plague. Young men who witness their proceedings admire them vastly as partners for the evening, but neither covet nor secure them as partners for life. Can they be blamed? Certainly not! They well know that girls who, at a dance, imbibe *freely* of the champagne cup and who, at a dinner party, drink as some few are in the habit of drinking, four or five or even six glasses of wine, — that such wives as these, if they ever do become mothers (which is very doubtful) will be mothers of a degenerate race. (1887)

Finger-Bowls. The fashion of finger-bowl and napkin would seem to commend itself to everybody as eminently cleanly and comfortable. Yet there are still well-to-do people who sneer at the idea of "doing one's washing at the table." (1906)

Napkins. "Mr. Blank has no napkin, James!" said a hostess of the nouveau riche order, to her butler.

"I beg pardon!" interposed the guest, lifting a corner of the napkin from his knee that she might see her mistake. "I have one."

"Ah!" with an apologetic smile. "I saw that you did not have it *on.*" Gentlemen are supposed to have put away bibs with other childish things. The suggestion of putting a napkin "on" is not agreeable. The place for the useful bit of linen is on the knee or lap, out of sight of fellow-eaters.

(1906)

Law of the Table is a respect to the common soul of all the guests. Everything is unseasonable which is private to two or three or any portion of the company. Tact never violates for a moment this law, never intrudes the orders of the house, the vices of the absent, or a tariff of expenses, or professional privacies; as we say, we never "talk shop" before company.

(1909)

GARNISHES

Decorate a crown roast by placing drained, spiced apples on the ends of the bone. Surround the roast with curly endive or whipped potatoes piped onto the platter with a pastry bag.

For luncheons, cut a cucumber in half crosswise and carefully remove the seeds. Fill with your favorite cheese spread and slice ½" thick. Make a stem out of a thin slice of green pepper and leaves from mint or any other herb and arrange on vegetable gelatin mold like a flower. Use a speck of pimento in the middle of the cucumber slice as the center of the flower. This could also decorate a salad.

Scallion Brushes. Slice the green end of a scallion off so that the entire scallion is about 4" long. Trim the end from the white part. Cut through the white end of the scallion approximately 1¼" lengthwise. Cut again perpendicular to the first cut another 1¼". Submerge in ice water and refrigerate. The ends will curl up.

Garnish fish with lemon wedges coated with freshly chopped parsley.

Serve chicken or shrimp salad in grapefruit shells with edges cut in scallop shapes with a sharp knife.

Hollow out cherry tomatoes and stuff with softened, whipped cream cheese piped into the tomatoes with a pastry bag.

Top lettuce or spinach salads with fresh mushrooms sliced in a hard-boiled egg slicer. Even slices every time.

For decorative ice cubes in drinks, boil the water for cubes first to eliminate air in frozen cubes and place cherries, sprigs of mint, small lemon peel twists, etc. in trays of cooled boiled water and freeze.

To make decorative ice molds for punch bowls, arrange flowers or fruit in a thin layer of water at the bottom of a bundt pan or other mold. When fruit or flowers are frozen in place, fill with more water and continue freezing. Always boil the water used in molds to be assured of clear water. Unmold by dipping quickly in hot water.

For tomato roses, peel the tomato with a vegetable peeler starting at the top and continuing around to the bottom. Roll the peel into a rose shape.

Use apples for candleholders by cutting a hole big enough for the candle in the stem end of the apple.

To frost grapes or strawberries, dip in unbeaten egg white and dust with confectioner's sugar.

Decorate potato salad by placing slices of hard-boiled eggs on top with thin slices of pimento radiating from the egg slice to simulate the sun.

Serve lemon mousse in lemon shells. Select large lemons and remove a small slice from the bottom of the lemon so it will stand on its own. Cut off about ¾" from the top and carefully remove the pulp. Mound lemon mousse in shells & freeze.

Chocolate Leaves. Melt four ounces of semi-sweet chocolate bits in a microwave oven or in the top of a double boiler. With a narrow spatula or a knife, spread the melted chocolate on one side of non-poisonous leaves such as rose leaves. Do not put chocolate on stems. Place glazed leaves chocolate-side up on a waxed paper-lined cookie sheet and chill for at least two hours. When chocolate has hardened, peel away the leaves by pulling on the uncovered stem. Use the chocolate leaves to garnish iced cakes, cupcakes or in whipped cream toppings for puddings, mousse or pots de creme.

Use popcorn to garnish steaming mugs of tomato soup.

Pickle Fans. Slice thinly a medium-sized gherkin or pickle lengthwise to within ¼" of the end. Spread to form a fan.

Bowl for Crudites. Hollow out a red cabbage to make a beautiful bowl for your special raw vegetable dip.

Ginger Perkins
St. Louis, Missouri

HOW MUCH IT TAKES TO SERVE 50 PEOPLE

	SERVING	TOTAL AMOUNT
Beverages:		
Juices	½ cup	6½ quarts
Coffee	1 cup	1 to 1½ pounds
Tea	1 cup	2½ ounces
Dairy Products:		
Butter on table	1½ pats	1½ pounds
Cream		1 quart
Ice cream, bulk		2 gallons
Ice cream, brick		7 to 8 bricks
Milk	1 glass	2½ gallons
Meats:		
Beef, Swiss steak		16 pounds
Beef, meat loaf		10 pounds
Pork, baked ham		18 pounds
Pork, ham loaf		12 pounds
Chicken (dressed weight), creamed		18 pounds
Turkey or chicken, roasted		39 to 40 pounds
Salads:		
Cabbage slaw		8 pounds
Potato salad (potatoes)		13 pounds
Salad dressing		1½ to 2 cups
Vegetables:		
Mashed potatoes		1 peck
Canned vegetables		2 #10 cans

Mrs. E. Kasperson
Trenton, Missouri

U.S. and Metric Systems Equivalents

Liquid Measurements

2 cups	= ½ liter	½ cup	= 1/8 liter
1 cup	= ¼ liter	⅓ cup	= 1/15 liter
¾ cup	= 1/6 liter	¼ cup	= 1/16 liter
⅔ cup	= 1/7 liter		

Solid Measurements

Rice, 1 cup = 150 grams

Granulated sugar:						
1 cup	=	190 grams	½ cup	=	95 grams
⅔ cup	=	125 grams	¼ cup	=	50 grams
Flour:					
1 cup	=	140 grams	½ cup	=	70 grams (1 stick butter)
⅔ cup	=	100 grams	¼ cup	=	35 grams
Butter:					
2 cups	=	400 grams	½ cup	=	100 grams (1 stick butter)
1 cup	=	200 grams	¼ cup	=	50 grams

1 cup	=	240 ml			
½ cup	=	120 ml	¼ tsp.	=	1½ ml
⅓ cup	=	80 ml	1 quart	=	946 ml
¼ cup	=	60 ml	1 pint	=	473 ml
1 Tbl.	=	15 ml	1 pound	=	454 grams
1 tsp.	=	5 ml			

EQUIVALENTS

Apples	3 pounds	2 quarts	Nuts, chopped	1 pound	4 cups
Butter	2 sticks	1 cup	Potatoes	1 pound	4 medium
Cheese, grated	4 ounces	1 cup	Brown sugar	1 pound	2⅔ cups
Cottage Cheese	8 ounces	1 cup	Granulated sugar	1 pound	2 cups
Chocolate	1 ounce	1 square	Powdered sugar	1 pound	2½ cups
Ground coffee	1 pound	serves 40	Tomatoes	1 pound	4 medium
Lemon juice	1 ounce	2 tablespoons			

SUBSTITUTIONS

1 cup sugar = 1 cup powdered sugar or 1 cup brown sugar.
1 cup sour milk = 1 tablespoon distilled white vinegar + sweet milk to equal 1 cup.
1 cup whipping cream = 2 cups whipped cream
1 cup heavy cream = white of 1 egg whipped + 1 cup light cream, whipped separately and folded together.
1 cup butter = 7/8 cup lard.
1 cake compressed yeast = 1 packet active dry yeast.
1 square unsweetened baking chocolate = 3 tablespoons unsweetened cocoa + 1 tablespoon butter.
1 tablespoon cornstarch = 2 tablespoons flour.
A 9" round cake pan = a 9x9" square cake pan.
An 8" round pan = a 7x7" square cake pan.
1 cup cake flour = ¾ cup + 2 tablespoons all purpose flour + 2 tablespoons cornstarch.
1 cup molasses = 1 cup white, powdered or brown sugar. Reduce liquid in recipe.

Index

PARTICIPATING COUNTIES

American Cancer Society
Missouri Division, Inc.
P.O. Box 1066
Jefferson City, MO 65102

Please send me ______ copies of the 1982 SHOW ME MISSOURI COOKING FOR COMPANY COOKBOOK for a $6.00 donation per copy (plus $1.25 per copy for postage and handling).

I enclose an additional donation of $____________. Enclosed is my check or money order for $________________. (Please make checks payable to The American Cancer Society.)

Name ____

Address ____

City ______________________ State__________________Zip__________

I want to add to my SHOW ME MISSOURI COOKBOOK series. Please send me ________ copies of 1981 SHOW ME MISSOURI HERITAGE COOKBOOK for a $5.00 donation per copy (plus $1.25 postage and handling per copy).

American Cancer Society
Missouri Division, Inc.
P.O. Box 1066
Jefferson City, MO 65102

Please send me ______ copies of the 1982 SHOW ME MISSOURI COOKING FOR COMPANY COOKBOOK for a $6.00 donation per copy (plus $1.25 per copy for postage and handling).

I enclose an additional donation of $____________. Enclosed is my check or money order for $________________. (Please make checks payable to The American Cancer Society.)

Name ____

Address ____

City ______________________ State__________________Zip__________

I want to add to my SHOW ME MISSOURI COOKBOOK series. Please send me ________ copies of 1981 SHOW ME MISSOURI HERITAGE COOKBOOK for a $5.00 donation per copy (plus $1.25 postage and handling per copy).

Re-Order Additional Copies